Powered Ships

I: THE BEGINNINGS

RICHARD ARMSTRONG

ERNEST BENN LIMITED
LONDON & TONBRIDGE

First published 1975 by Ernest Benn Limited,
25 New Street Square, Fleet Street, London, EC4A 3JA

&

Sovereign Way, Tonbridge, Kent, TN9 1RW

Distributed in Canada by
The General Publishing Company Limited, Toronto

Maps by E. A. Chambers
Book designed by Kenneth Day

Printed in Great Britain

ISBN *0 510-12611-1*

1 The illustration on the title page shows John Fitch's second steamboat

CONTENTS

MAPS

2 Symington's original steam engine

3 '. . . they all need ships.'

I *Introduction*

IN THIS AGE OF MOON-LANDINGS and interplanetary probes, no one marvels any more about power-driven ships. We can, if so minded, still see them featured occasionally in travel agency brochures and glossy magazine advertisements which boast of their great size and speed, the opulence of their fittings, the extravagance of their cuisine and the variety of entertainment provided aboard them; but even the innocent and the pretentious who hopefully succumb to the ad-men's lure, have no wonder left in them for the ship herself. Her existence is accepted, along with that of the automobile, telecommunications and computers, as one of the basic elements in the structure of society.

Yet life without ships is inconceivable. Everybody depends on them in some degree. The men growing wheat on the Canadian prairies, rearing cattle in the Argentine, raising sheep in Australia and New Zealand, producing oil in the Middle East or Venezuela, culling timber in the rain forests of Africa and the pinewoods of North America, wresting mineral ores from deposits in the earth's desert places – they all need ships, not only to carry the products of their enterprise to the ultimate consumer, but also to supply themselves with the necessities and luxuries they cannot produce. And without ships, the thickly peopled, highly industrialized areas of the world could not for long survive in their present form. Ships bring them the major part of their daily bread and the meat they eat with it, as well as a wide variety of fruit, fresh and dried, spices and flavourings, tea, coffee and cocoa and such exotic food-grains as rice, millet, rape-seed, maize and soya beans. Ships supply them with the wool, cotton and other fibres that feed their textile industries, the timber with which they build and furnish their homes, the basic raw materials for all their consumer durables from washing machines to motor cars, and the petroleum products to nourish the convoluted chemicals and plastics plants and fuel the now totally mechanized transport systems. 'Swift shuttles', Kipling called them in his day, and, as the 'loom' they work becomes ever more complex and sophisticated, they multiply at a staggering rate. Thus, in its annual summary, *Lloyd's Register of Shipping* gives the total of new ships launched throughout the world in 1971 as 24,859,701 tons, representing an increase on the previous year's production of 3,170,188 tons (*The Times*, 24 February 1972).

Yet, just over a hundred years ago, the powered ship was still in the process of coming into being. Grossly inefficient, cripplingly uneconomic and, in the main, grimly ugly, it was struggling to establish itself against the competition of the sailing ship, then at its peak in both performance and heart-stopping romantic beauty. In terms of world gross tonnage afloat, even as late as 1860, there was roughly seven tons of sailing ship to every one of steamer. The actual figures were: sailing ships 8,707,105; steamships 1,351,800 (Lindsay, iv, app. 27, p. 646) and it is important to note that a considerable proportion of the steamship tonnage – perhaps between 10 and 15 per cent – was designed for operation on lakes and inland waterways and not for the intercontinental trades.

A century before that, the power-driven ship was no more than a dream: the wishful thinking of successive generations of cranks and visionaries.

To those immediately involved in its development and growth, the dream brought more heartache than happiness, for every success was achieved at the expense of someone's failure, each step forward made on the wreckage of other men's hopes. Moreover, as the project became more and more demonstrably viable, men moved by urges other than the ultimate good of all took a hand in it and personal ambition, national pride and plain unvarnished greed came into the reckoning to bedevil the designers and confuse the dedicated planners. But in the long run the dreamers triumphed: to the inestimable benefit of all mankind. The powered ship opened up the world, peopled its empty places and made its riches potentially available to all.

2 *Experiment*

THE INVENTORS

The magic-makers

THE IDEA OF PROPELLING a boat by means other than toil and sweat, goes further back than written history to the time when man invented the sail. That simple device released him from the drudgery of the paddle and the slavery of the oar, but left him at the mercy of head winds and adverse currents and it would be about then that he started to dream up ways of winning free. The earliest known record of an attempt to achieve this end is found in Morisotus, *Orbis Maritima*, published in 1643. It suggests that the paddle-wheel as a mode of propelling ships was known to the ancients, and the writer claims to have seen a bas-relief showing an Illyrian galley so driven, the wheels being turned by a team of oxen working on a treadmill. Doubt, however, is now cast on the authenticity of this interpretation of these antique works of art, though Lindsay declares that in the nineteenth century one such craft was plying as a ferryboat on the St Lawrence, and in England another ran for some time between Yarmouth and Norwich.

Disbelief is also the ultimate lot of Blasco de Garay of Barcelona. The story goes that in 1543, he petitioned the Emperor Charles V for permission to construct an engine which would propel 'large ships in calm without the use of sails or oars'. In spite of strenuous opposition from religious and other quarters, he was given the go-ahead and the loan of a ship for the purpose of his experiment. She was the *Trinity*, a vessel of 200 tons burden lying in the port of Barcelona with a full cargo of grain, and on 17 June 1543, he practised his mystery aboard her. Mystery it was and remained, for de Garay kept his machinery under cover and refused to exhibit it to the public. Contemporary accounts describe it as consisting of a cauldron of boiling water and two wheels, set in motion by it, which revolved externally on either side of the ship. They suggest the project was

4 Primitive paddle-boats. From Valturius' *De Re Militari*, 1472

abandoned partly because the speed attained was no more than two leagues in three hours but mainly because of fear that the boiler would burst. De Garay dismantled his machine still unseen and after dispersing the several parts of it, was promoted and given a grant of money for his trouble.

In 1857 the story of de Garay was very thoroughly investigated by John MacGregor, a barrister-at-law, who found no evidence to support it and numerous reasons to doubt it. In a paper read at the Society of Arts on 14 April 1858, he demolished the claim. De Garay, he said, carried out the experiment aboard the *Trinity*, but instead of a steam engine under the covers, he had twenty-five men on each side of the ship driving the paddle-wheels either by a capstan or some form of treadmill. The boiler, one assumes, was a piece of stage property.

So much for the early and what might be called the apocryphal attempts. Those that follow are documented and can be checked.

In effect, the problem had by this time broken down into three basic requirements, namely: (*a*) a source of continuous power; (*b*) an engine with which to control that power and convert it into continuous motion; and (*c*) a method of applying that motion to the work of driving a ship.

The requisite power had been there under everybody's nose as it were, for upwards of 2,000 years. It was, of course, steam and Hero, a philosopher-mathematician living in Alexandria was experimenting with it about 120 BC. He also wrote about it and in his book, *On Pneumatics*, an edition of which was published by a Mr Woodcroft in London in 1851, he describes his apparatus and the results it gave him:

> Let a fire be lighted under a cauldron with water in it, and covered with a lid; and attach to this cauldron a bent tube with the extremity fitting into a hollow ball. Opposite to the extremity of this tube place a pivot fastened to the lid, and let the ball have various tubes communicating with it at opposite ends of the diameter, with their bendings at right angles [i.e. in opposite directions]. Then when the fire is lighted, the steam passing through the first tube [i.e. from the cauldron] into the ball will pass out through the bent tubes towards the lid, causing the ball to revolve after the fashion of dancing figures.
>
> [quoted Lindsay, iv, p. 6]

This machine, which he called the *Aeolipile*, was no more than a laboratory experiment, an amusing toy or a priest's mystery; but it demonstrated the force inherent in steam and, at the very least, hinted at the principle of the steam turbine.

5 Reconstruction of Hero's *Aeolipile*

Samuel Morland, 1625–95

The nature of steam is now more widely understood but there are still some popular misconceptions about it. Scientists describe it as a dry, colourless and transparent, gaseous substance created when water is vaporized by heat. The wet, white cloud emerging from a boiling kettle or a locomotive's exhaust system is not steam but small droplets of water formed when it comes into contact with the surrounding colder atmosphere and condenses. Thus with a boiling kettle, there is always a gap between the end of the spout and the beginning of the vapour cloud and the warmer the ambient air, the bigger that gap will be. Leaving aside for the moment superheated steam which approximately obeys the laws governing the expansion of gases, the specific volume of steam is very much greater than that of water. The comparative figures at 100 °Centigrade – i.e. boiling point – are: water 0·017 cubic foot per lb.; steam 26·8 cubic feet per lb.; or to put it another way, steam occupies 1,600 times the space of an equal weight of water. It is this characteristic that, one way or another, constitutes the power inherent in steam.

The first man to record this phenomenon was Sir Samuel Morland, Master of Works to Charles II. In a paper preserved in the Harleian Collection at the British Museum and entitled *The Principles of the New Force of Fire, invented by Samuel Morland in 1682, and presented to His Most Christian Majesty in 1683*, he wrote:

> . . . water being converted into vapour by the force of fire, these vapours shall require a greater space (about 2000 times) than the water occupied, and sooner than be constantly confined would split a piece of canon.
>
> [quoted Lindsay, iv, p. 24]

He was out, of course, but not significantly so and he laid a foundation of knowledge on which others were able to build.

Denis Papin, *c.* 1647–1712

One of these was Denis Papin, a French physicist born at Blois. The popular story is that Papin built himself a steam pumping engine and in 1707 adapted it to drive a model boat on the River Fulda. The local boatmen, reared to oar and sail, and seeing the little craft as a device of the devil or a threat to their livelihood, destroyed it in the

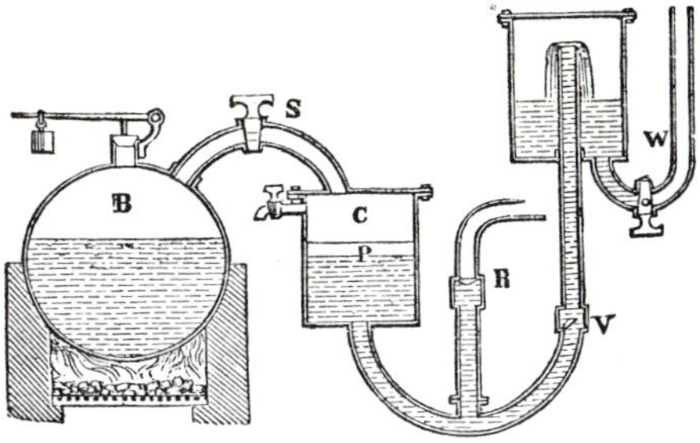

6a Papin's steam pump. B, boiler; S, cock; C, cylinder; P, piston; R, feed-pipe; V, non-return valves; W, outlet

6b Denis Papin

night and forced the inventor to fly for his life. But there was much more to Papin than this implies. He was a Huguenot and did indeed flee France after the Edict of Nantes giving security and civil rights to the sect, had ceased to function. Settling in England, he became a member of the Royal Society and was, for a period its secretary. He was associated with Robert Boyle in his researches into the properties of air, especially in regard to its elasticity, compressibility and weight.

Papin's most important contribution to the development of the steam engine was the recognition that if water converted to steam increased its volume many hundred times, it followed that steam reconverted to water must shrink into something like its original dimensions and, in an airtight container, create a vacuum. To demonstrate this fact, he invented a method of condensing steam in a cylinder.

Thomas Newcomen, 1663–1729

Long before this, however, the steam engine had begun to take shape, at least in the minds of inventors; and in 1618, David Ramsay obtained a patent for a device 'to make boates for carriages running upon the water as swift in calmes and more safe in storms than boats full sayled in great windes. . . .' And again in 1630, he patented a scheme '. . . to make boats, ships, and barges to goe against the wind and tide . . . and to raise water from lowe pitts by fire.'

Ramsay sank into obscurity but others were ready to take up the torch and in 1637, Francis Lis patented a plan:

> . . . to use and exercise upon the River Thames, and any other river within England and Wales, according to their own way and inventing the sole drauinge and workinge up of all Barges and other vessels without the use of horses.

He was followed in 1648 by Edward Ford, who proposed a plan for the navigation of rivers whereby he could:

> . . . bring little ships, barges, and vessels in and out of havens without or against any small wynde or tide and transport souldiers and passengers without or against wynde yf the seas be not rough. . . .

Then came Thomas Grant, Doctor of Physic, who obtained a patent:

> . . . for several instruments, whereof the first is an instrument very profitable when comon winds fayle for a more speedy passage of calmed shipps or other vessels upon the sea or great rivers, which may be called the wynds maty. . . .

And in 1661 the aristocracy took a hand when the Marquis of Worcester was credited with an invention:

> . . . applicable to make a boat that roweth or letteth, even against wind and stream to any part of the compass which way so ever the stream runs or wind blows, and yet the force of the wind or stream causeth its motion. . . .

The above quotations, all from Woodcroft's *Specifications of Marine Propulsion*, are repeated by Lindsay who states categorically that in spite of all that has been said about James Watt, the Marquis of Worcester '. . . was the first to make an *actual* steam-engine' [vol. iv. fn. p. 18].

Like Ramsay, most of these early inventors seem to have seen the device primarily as a new kind of pump for freeing mines of water, and this was certainly what Thomas Savery was seeking. Savery, born in 1650, was a military engineer who gave himself up to the study of mechanics and in 1696 he invented a machine 'for raising water and occasioning motion to all sorts of mill-work by the impelling force of *Fire*'. Six years after that, in a paper which he entitled the *Miners' Friend*, he suggested his pump '. . . may be very useful to

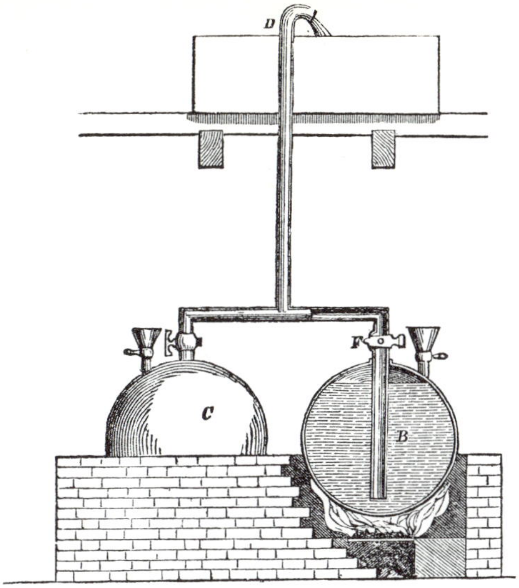

7a Worcester's engine

7b Marquis of Worcester

ships, but I dare not meddle with that matter, and leave it to the judgement of those who are the best judges of maritime affairs.'

Savery's pump was short on power and quickly superseded; but his contribution was significant and no less an authority than Lindsay credits him with 'having constructed the first *really practicable* steam-engine' [iv, p. 25].

The man who took the flickering torch from Savery was Thomas Newcomen, a working blacksmith of Dartmouth. He had nothing to do with ships but in 1705, in association with Savery and John Calley, he took out a patent for what he called a 'fire-engine' which is now identified as the *atmospheric steam engine*. In essence, it consisted of a cylinder within which a piston was moved to and fro by steam alternately admitted through one valve and expelled through another. A rod on the piston was connected to a beam, imparting to it a rocking motion which worked a pump.

The device exploited the vacuum created by condensation of the steam in the closed cylinder. At first this effect was achieved by applying cooling water to the outside of the cylinder, but this was a

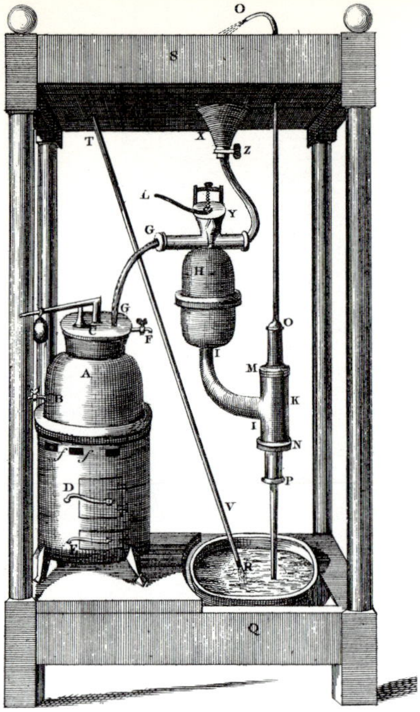

8 Savery's engine. B, boiler; GG, steampipe; C, gauge-pipe; H, receiver; L, manually operated valve; I, sucking pipe; R, well; OO, forcing pipe; NP, valves; S, reservoir; XYZ, condenser jet

slow process and with it the piston strokes came at very long intervals. Consequently, after some heart-searching, the engine was modified and condensation effected by throwing a jet of water directly into the cylinder. The engine in its final form functioned as follows (see illustration No. 9):

> **B** is the boiler from which steam passes through the pipe **D** into the cylinder **C**, equalising its internal pressure with that of the atmosphere, at which point the heavy pump-rod **k** falls, tilting the beam which thus raises the piston attached to its other end to the top of its stroke. The cock at **D** is then shut and a jet of water from the cistern **g** injected into the cylinder through the cock **Z** to produce a vacuum by the condensation of the steam. The pressure of the air above the piston now forces it down, again raising the pump-rods and thus the engine works on indefinitely. The condensing water together with the water of condensation flows off through the open pipe.
>
> [adapted from Thurston, p. 59]

The original engine made 6 to 8 strokes per minute; the improved version 10 to 12. As usual with inventors, Newcomen used the discoveries and built on the work of his predecessors, adapting Papin's cylinder and piston and developing Savery's method of condensation,

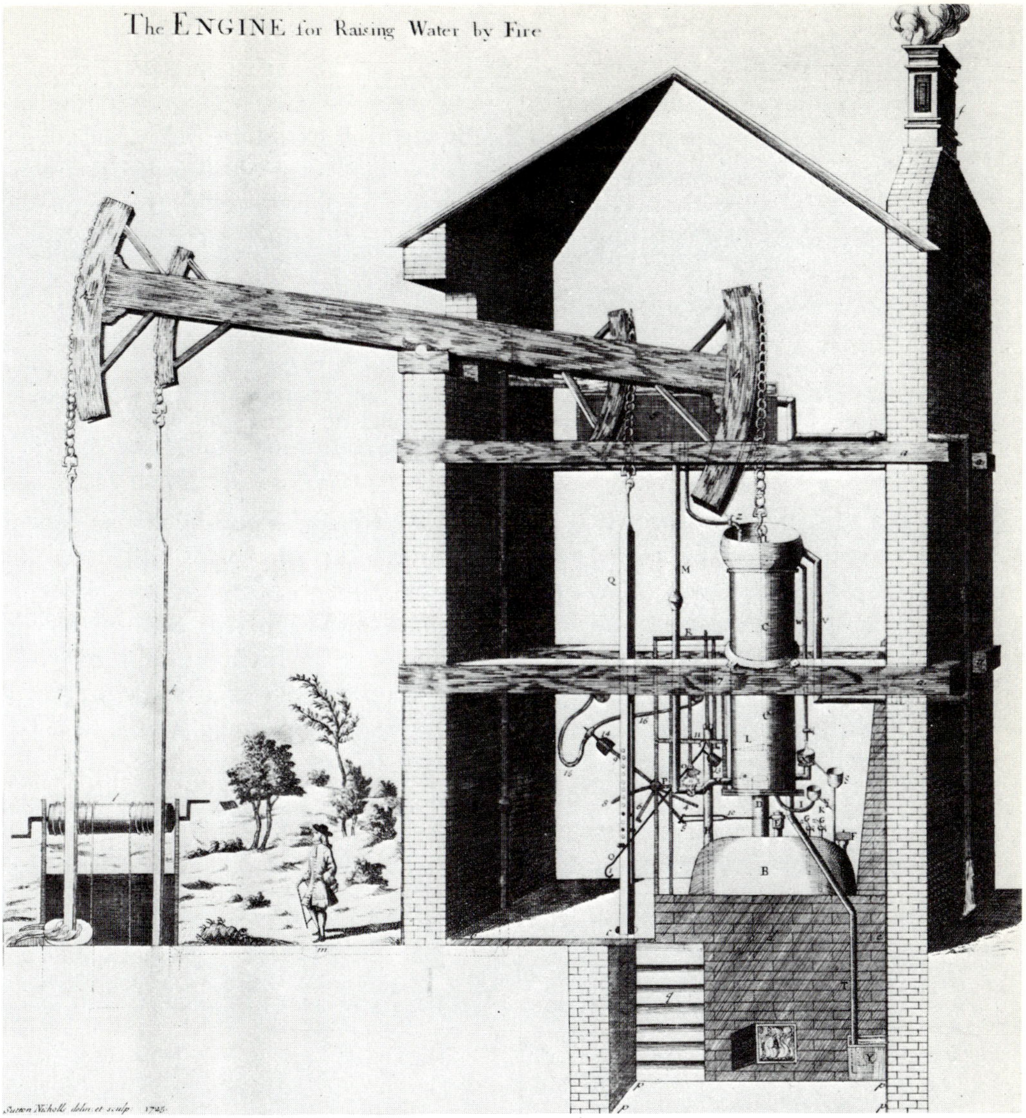

9 Newcomen's engine in mid-stroke

then adding the overhead beam with the piston-rod at one end and the pump-rod at the other. The engine was claimed to combine great safety with economy and in 1723 it was set up at Griff, near Coventry and used for drawing water.

Jonathan Hulls

Newcomen's engine, unlike its predecessors, worked, and a few years later, Jonathan Hulls, no doubt inspired by its success, tried to adapt it for driving a tugboat. Hulls was born at Campden in Gloucestershire in 1699 and made his first experiments on the Avon at Evesham. In December 1736, he secured a patent for a 'machine for carrying ships and vessels out of or into any harbour or river against wind and tide or in a calm. . . .' According to Woodcroft, Hulls

> . . . placed a paddle-wheel on beams projecting over the stern, and it was turned by an atmospheric steam-engine acting in conjunction with a counterpoise weight upon a system of ropes and grooved wheels. . . .
> [quoted Lindsay iv, p. 26]

His specification described a method of driving a paddle-wheel by converting a reciprocating rectilinear motion into a continuous rotary one. The idea was new and ingenious, but too complicated for successful commercial development and, although this is the first steamboat authentically recorded, there is no evidence that it ever got off the drawing-board. Nevertheless Hulls persevered and in 1737 published a pamphlet entitled *A Description and Draughts of a New Invented Machine*, in which he proposed to use a Newcomen steam engine to drive a stern paddle-wheel aboard a tugboat. This idea also apparently died still-born, and the power-driven ship remained just a dream haunting the minds of men for another half a century or so.

10 Tugboat proposed by Jonathan Hulls, 1736

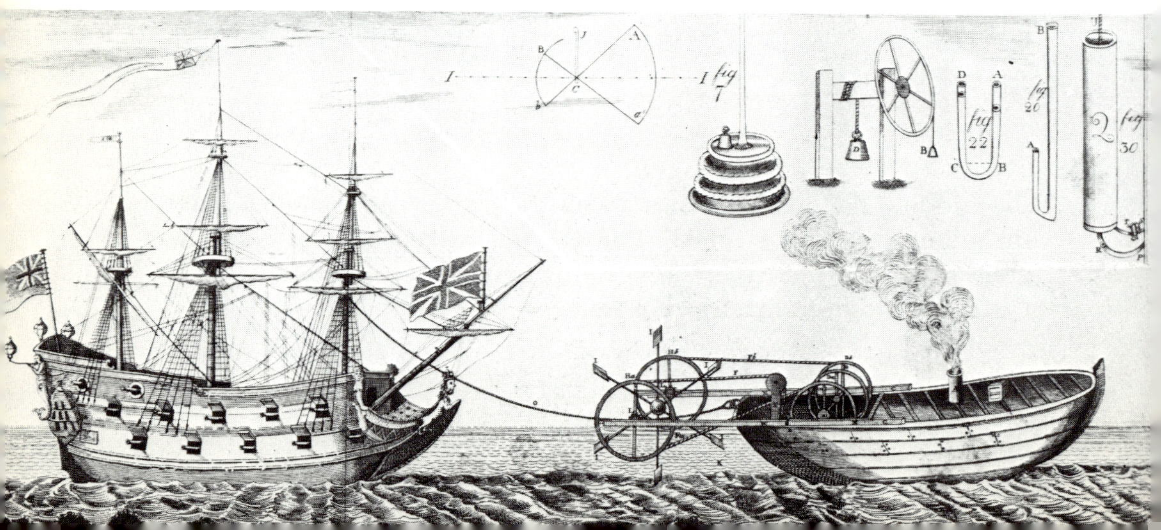

There were a number of reasons for this. In the first place, in spite of Newcomen's extravagant claims and the brilliance of the idea behind it, his engine was extremely inefficient. There were problems connected with the conversion of the reciprocating motion of the engine into a continuous rotary movement that could be applied to a paddle-wheel; and the tools, techniques and even materials available for the solution of these practical difficulties, were crude and unequal to the task. Finally, the theoretical knowledge of such subjects as combustion, thermodynamics, and kinetics, was either scanty, erroneous, or totally non-existent.

But the second half of the eighteenth century was a time of great political, economic and social change, to keep pace with which some major break-through in the method and scope of available transportation was urgently needed. In England the Industrial Revolution was getting into its stride; on the Continent there was growing unrest among the masses of the people, and all over the known world the demand for a wider, richer, fuller life was becoming more insistent. Men wanted to go places; to develop new ideas and exchange them, to meet each other for discussion and mutual enlightenment; and above all, they wanted to trade – to take abroad their surplus manufactures and exchange them for an ever-widening range of raw materials and the products of different countries and other cultures.

All this demanded better, faster and more regular communication between producer and consumer, merchant and supplier, the mother country and her colonial possessions.

There were mail services of a kind, it is true. In 1633 a *ship pacquet* service had been set up in England and letters were carried across the Channel either by rowing-boat or sailing lugger. The difficulty of maintaining a regular mail service by sea beyond the confines of the English Channel lay in the fact that the wind in the area was predominantly westerly and it was a common experience for ships outward bound to spend days, even weeks, beating to seaward against it or laying up in a south coast port waiting for a favourable shift. In 1688, Falmouth was made the port of departure for mails to the Iberian Peninsula and the Mediterranean, as ships were able to leave there even with a westerly gale blowing and still get a slant to the southward. This eased the situation to some extent, but the

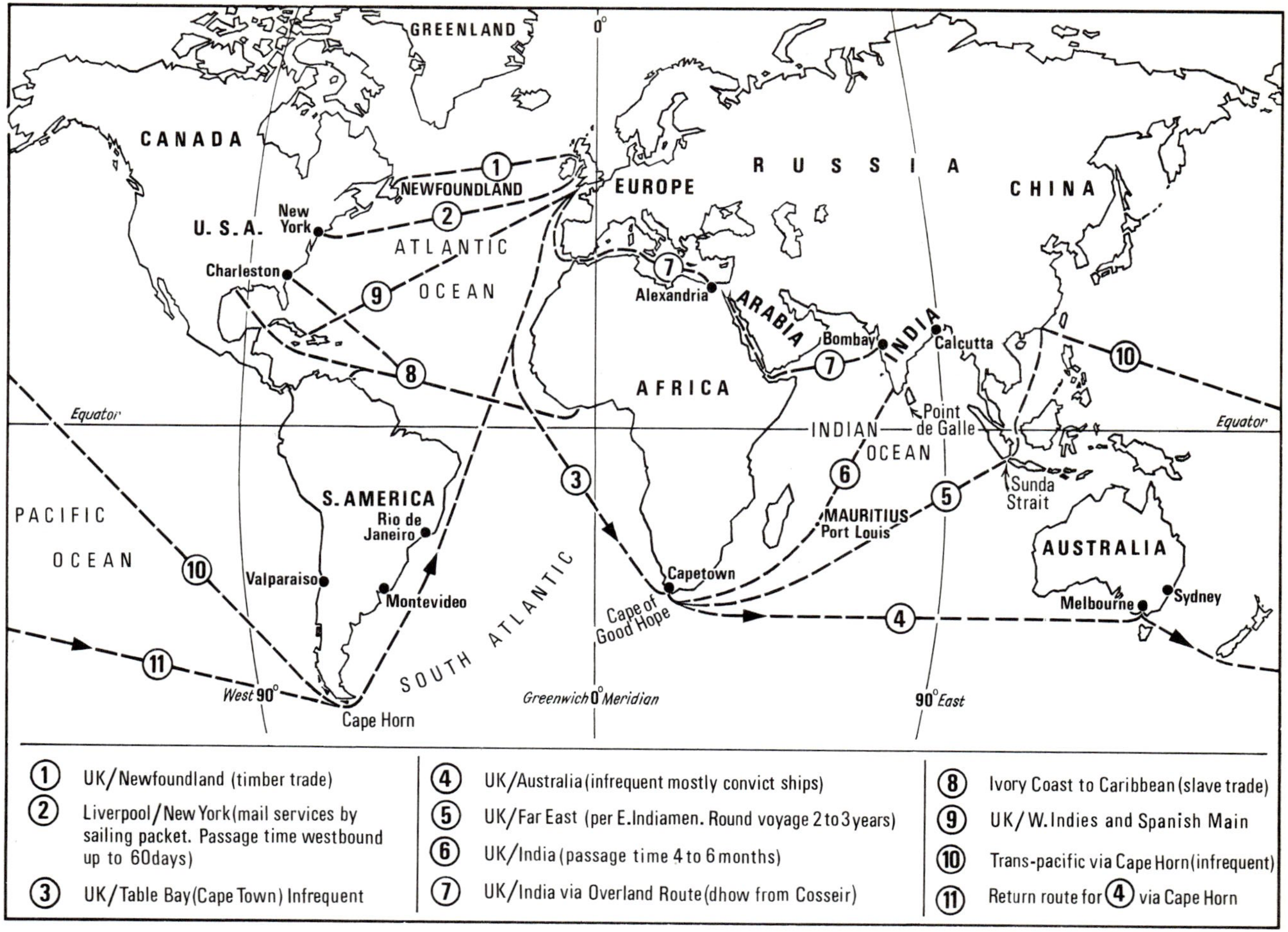

MAP No. 1 The world showing trade routes and main lines of communication *c.* 1800

services remained slow and irregular. A letter to America could take anything up to two months on the crossing; and a round trip in an Indiaman via the Cape still took, not months but years, off a man's life.

In these circumstances, there was a growing pressure on inventive minds to translate the dream of powered ships, independent of wind and tide, into practical reality, and as usual, history threw up a man to fit the need. His name was James Watt.

Watt was born at Greenock in Scotland in 1736 and at the age of twenty-one, he became mathematical instrument-maker to Glasgow University. Extremely able and enormously busy, Watt made a significant contribution to wide areas of civil and mechanical engineering. He did a great deal of work in connection with the construction of canals, especially the Caledonian and that linking the Forth and Clyde estuaries; he was concerned with the deepening of rivers and the improvement of such harbours as Ayr, Port Glasgow and Greenock; but he is best remembered for his contribution to the development of the steam engine.

There is some evidence that he began thinking of steam as a motive force quite early in his career; consequently Newcomen's pumping engine had special interest for him. In 1764, he made a detailed study of it which resulted in several important discoveries about steam. Among them were: (*a*) that a very small quantity of steam is required to heat a very large quantity of water; (*b*) the existence of *latent heat* – an idea new to him although it had already been demonstrated by Joseph Black; (*c*) that at boiling point, steam when condensing, is capable of heating six times the weight of water which was used for producing condensation; and (*d*) that steam, weight for weight, is a vastly greater absorbent and reservoir of heat than water. His final conclusion was that not less than 75 per cent of the heat supplied to Newcomen's engine was wasted. He said:

> When analysed, the invention would not appear so great as it seemed to be. In the state in which I found the steam-engine, it was no great effort of mind to observe that the quantity of fuel necessary to make it work would forever prevent its extensive utility. The next step in my progress was equally easy – to inquire what was the cause of the great consumption of fuel. This, too, was readily suggested, viz., the waste of fuel which was necessary to bring the whole cylinder, piston, and adjacent parts from the coldness of water to the heat of steam, no fewer than from 15 to 20 times in a minute. [quoted Smiles, *Lives of Boulton and Watt*]

From this starting-point, James Watt proceeded to change the atmospheric engine of Newcomen into the modern steam engine. To put it in the simplest possible way, his aim was to keep the engine at all stages of its operation, as hot as the steam entering it; and he achieved this end by introducing a steam jacket round the cylinder and a separate condenser. The first engine of the new type was built at Kinneil. Its cylinder was 18 inches in diameter and Thurston describes its operation as follows:

> . . . the steam passes from the boiler through the pipe *d* and the valve *c* to the cylinder-casing or steam-jacket, *yy*, and above the piston, *b*, which it follows in its descent in the cylinder, *a*, the valve *f* being at this time open, to allow the exhaust into the condenser, *h*.
>
> The piston now being at the lower end of the cylinder, and the pump-rods at the opposite end of the beam, *y*, being thus raised and the pump filled with water, the valves *c* and *f* close, while *e* opens, allowing the steam which remains above the piston to flow beneath it, until, the pressures becoming equal above and below, the weight of the pump-rods overbalancing that of the piston, the latter is rapidly drawn to the top of the cylinder, while the steam is displaced above, passing to the underside of the piston.
>
> The valve *e* is next closed, and *c* and *f* are again opened; the down-stroke is repeated. The water and air entering the condenser are removed at each stroke by the air-pump, *i*, which communicates with the condenser by the passage *s*. The pump *q* supplies condensing-water, and the pump *A* takes away a part of the water of condensation, which is thrown by the air-pump into the 'hot-well,' *k*, and from it the feed-pump supplies the boiler. The valves are moved by valve-gear very similar to Beighton's and Smeaton's, by the pins, *mm*, in the 'plug-frame' or 'tappet-rod,' *nn*.
>
> The engine is mounted upon a substantial foundation, *BB*. *F* is an opening out of which before starting the engine, the air is driven from the cylinder and condenser.
>
> [Thurston, pp. 98–9]

The patent covering these improvements was granted on 5 January 1769 and from that date the steamship, though still a long way off, was a practical possibility. Watt's next move was to enter into partnership with a Mr Matthew Boulton, who owned the Soho Ironworks near Birmingham and undertook the manufacture of what then became famous as the Boulton and Watt Steam Engine.

Among the various improvements covered by Watt's patent, was the method of causing the steam to act above the piston, as well as below it, hence the description of the Boulton and Watt Steam Engine as *double-acting*.

11 James Watt's engine, 1774

12 Principle of double-acting engine. M, boiler, a and b, steam inlets; c and d, steam exits to condenser I; when a and c are opened steam operates above piston, P, forcing it down as steam below it condenses. Then as a and c shut, b and d open and the process is repeated below the piston

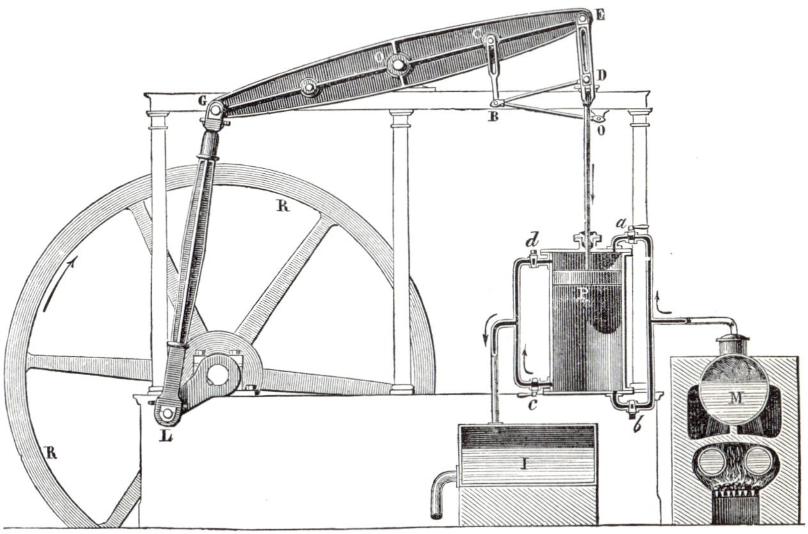

is a circumstance of much importance. This apparatus for working the ship is fixed in or beyond the stern in or about the place where the rudder is usually placed, and its movement is occasioned by means of a horizontal spindle or axletree conveyed to the engine through the stern end of the ship. . . . [quoted Lindsay, iv, pp. 31–2]

Muirhead, however, claims that James Watt suggested the screw as a means of driving ships fifteen long years before Bramah thought of it. He may well have done so, but there is no denying that his steam engine was designed for use on land and the idea of adapting it to drive ships first occurred to an American. It was William Henry who as early as 1770 was inspired by it to construct a number of model boats at Lancaster, Pennsylvania. None of them worked, but the experiments bore fruit, for among those watching them were John Fitch and Robert Fulton, both famous visionaries.

John Fitch, 1743–98

There has always been an element of tragedy in the continuing story of steam navigation and it is exemplified by John Fitch, who knew it all – the high hopes repeatedly dashed, the ridicule, the rejection, the erosion of resources, material and spiritual, resulting in poverty and the ultimate despair.

Fitch was born in Connecticut on 21 January 1743, the son of a small farmer who apprenticed him to a watch- and clock-maker. He appears to have been a rather restless soul and after working for some time as a silversmith at Trenton, New Jersey, became armourer to the State of New Jersey during the War of Independence. There is also a record of him functioning as a sutler, in which capacity he supplied the American camp at Valley Forge with goods and provisions. Finally, he did some land surveying and while so occupied became interested in the idea of using the steam engine to drive wheeled vehicles. Instead of pursuing this project, however, he turned his mind to propelling boats by steam on the rivers of the United States. His vision was prophetic and while trying to raise money for his schemes he wrote to a Mr David Rettenhouse as follows:

This, sir, whether I bring it to perfection or not, will be the mode of crossing the Atlantic in time for packets and armed vessels.

[quoted Lindsay, iv, p. 45]

14 Fitch's first steamboat on the Delaware River, USA

In 1785 James Rumsey and John Fitch obtained from the Legislature of Virginia and Maryland the exclusive right to run steamboats on the waters of those States; and in the following year, Fitch himself was granted similar rights by the States of New York and Pennsylvania. By this time Fitch's dream had taken shape in the form of a boat 34 feet long which was driven, not by a paddle-wheel, but by 12 vertical oars like outsize shovels to which the power of the steam engine was transmitted through a chain drive and a geared sprocket-wheel. The vessel was tried out at Shepherdstown,

Pennsylvania and attained a speed, it is said, of 4 or 5 miles an hour against the current on the Potomac.

A second and bigger boat was produced in 1787. She was 45 feet long with a 12-foot beam and her power-unit was a steam cylinder 12 inches in diameter. The *New York Magazine* for 1790 reported that this new craft made the trip from Philadelphia to Burlington at an average rate of 6 or 7 miles an hour. In 1790 a third boat was built, this time a 60-footer, and a company was formed to exploit the wonderful new invention.

Accounts differ about actual dates, but agree that somewhere around 1790, twelve substantial citizens of Philadelphia made the 20-mile trip to Burlington in one of Fitch's boats and afterwards issued a statement which declared among other things:

> . . . we are clearly of opinion that the rivers of America may be navigated by means of steamboats and that the present boat would be very useful on the Western Waters. . . .

And the *Federal Gazette and Philadelphia Advertiser* of 26 July 1790 carried the following notice:

> The steam-boat sets out to-morrow morning at ten o'clock from Arch Street Ferry, in order to take passengers for Burlington, Bristol, Bordingtown and Fenton.

This would seem to exclude any doubt that Fitch's boat actually traded with passengers on the Delaware; but the inventor himself did not follow up the line of steam service he had established and the assumption is that his machinery was too complicated and the cost of running it too great to show a profit.

Fitch continued to dream and talk about steamboats. He wrote:

> The grand and Principle Object, must be the Atlantick, which would soon over-spread the wild forests of America with people, and make us the most opulent Empire on Earth.

What he envisaged did indeed come to pass and in full measure; but he saw none of it, not even the beginning. For him everything failed and all he had was the heartbreak. He wandered the streets of Philadelphia, 'a figure of pity to some and scorn to others', and the consensus of opinion was that steamboats had driven him out of his mind. He died, by his own hand it is said, in 1798.

That was in America and one of the strangest circumstances in the history of steam navigation is that while John Fitch was proving it to be a practical proposition on his side of the Atlantic, Patrick Miller and William Symington were doing precisely the same thing on the other.

The *Charlotte Dundas*, 1801

Patrick Miller (1731–1815) was an Edinburgh banker with a passion for ships. He had ideas for propelling boats with a paddle-wheel powered by men walking round a capstan and is reputed to have spent £30,000 on abortive experiments before he was put in touch with Symington. Then began a collaboration that produced what Kirkcaldy calls 'the first successful steamer capable of doing service either in the carriage of passengers or goods. . . .' William Symington (1763–1831), son of a Lanarkshire mining engineer, was an expert mechanic. On 5 June 1787 he took out a patent for a new type of steam engine originally intended for propelling wheeled carriages. This device he undertook to fit into a boat belonging to Miller, whose employee rather than partner he had become.

The engine, newly built, was mounted in an oak frame and set up on the deck of a craft 25 feet long and 7 feet wide. The engine's cylinder was only 4 inches in diameter but, when tried on Loch Dalswinton, it drove the boat at a speed of 5 miles an hour and was considered an outstanding success. That was on 14 October 1788, and after a few more runs on the lake, the engine was taken out of the boat and set up as an ornamental curiosity in Miller's home, a double engine with 18-inch cylinders being ordered from the Carron Iron Works to replace it. In November 1789 the second engine was tried and drove the boat at a speed of 7 miles per hour.

At this point Mr Miller, having reached the bottom of his purse, or decided that one way and another he had put enough into the project, gave it up and Symington was left looking for another patron. Ten years he spent looking in vain and then, in 1801, he made contact with Lord Dundas, who engaged him to construct a steamboat for the Forth and Clyde Canal Company in which he was a large shareholder.

After studying the improvements introduced by James Watt and

15 Miller and Symington's experimental steamboat on Loch Dalswinton, 1788

others, Symington produced an entirely new engine which he patented on 14 March 1801. To some extent it was a compilation rather than an invention from scratch, not only using the steam on both sides of the piston which was Watt's patent but also incorporating Pickard's connecting-rod and crank and Miller's improved paddle-wheel. This machinery was fitted into the *Charlotte Dundas*, a vessel named after His Lordship's daughter, which, in spite of Fitch's earlier labours in the field, is generally accepted as *the first practical steamboat*.

The *Charlotte Dundas* was a stern-wheeler, with a double-acting engine. The single cylinder was horizontal, 22 inches in diameter and the piston had a stroke of 4 feet. It was coupled by a connecting-rod, directly on to the crankshaft of the paddle-wheel and as a power-plant was both simple and effective, virtues very rare indeed at that time. Commercially she was successful, towing two barges carrying 70 tons each on the Forth and Clyde Canal; but objections were raised to her continued use because it was feared the wash she made would damage the banks of the canal and further development was blocked for a time. Nevertheless the *Charlotte Dundas* was

16 The *Charlotte Dundas* on the Forth and Clyde Canal, 1801

seminal and her engine was for many years the standard pattern used in steam vessels. Consequently, Symington has been called 'the father of marine engineering' and his contribution to steam navigation is equated with that of Richard Trevithick to railways.

He got little joy out of its success, however, though the immediate prospects looked fair enough. Lord Dundas was so pleased with the vessel, he recommended the adoption of Symington's system to the Duke of Bridgewater who expressed a desire to have eight similar boats constructed for use on his own canal. Then before a binding agreement could be made, the Duke died and his successors cancelled the order, fearing like the Scots, that the wash of a steamboat would break down the banks of a canal. The *Charlotte Dundas* was laid up in a creek off the canal near Bramford Drawbridge where, Lindsay tells us, '. . . she remained for many years exposed to public view, as a curiosity – doubtless also as a warning to speculators!'

Symington, like Fitch, fell on hard times. In 1825 being almost penniless, he petitioned the Government of the day for a pension and the Treasury awarded him £100 as a gift from the Privy Purse with another £50 to follow later. He died a pauper.

'Fulton's Folly', 1807

Meanwhile in America, other experimenters were carrying on from where Fitch had left off. Notable among them were Colonel John Cox Stevens (1749–1838) and Robert Fulton (1765–1815). Stevens was a long way ahead in his thinking and in 1804 he produced the *Little Juliana*, a vessel 24 feet long equipped with a single-cylinder non-condensing engine. The engine, exhausting into the atmosphere, was a step backwards, but he made up for that by using high-pressure steam generated in a *multi-tubular boiler* and driving with it *twin-screw propellers* – ideas not generally adopted till more than half a century later.

The *Little Juliana* puffed around New York harbour at the dizzy speed of 4 miles an hour and Stevens was so entranced with his novel means of propulsion that he went on working at it for years. But, like so many of the dreamers, he was frustrated by lack of suitable tools and workmen sufficiently skilled to put his plans into effect. In the end he declared that after spending $20,000 and thirteen of the best years of his life on the project, he had to admit that his attempts were on the whole unsuccessful. Nevertheless, he is credited with one other notable achievement. In 1808 he built the paddle-steamer *Phoenix*, which was the first steamboat ever to make a passage in the open sea. His sons, Robert Livingstone Stevens (1787–1856) and Edwin Augustus Stevens (1795–1868) both devoted their lives to pioneering steam navigation in the United States of America.

Robert Fulton, contemporary of the Colonel and perhaps more widely known, has been described as '. . . an artist of high merit, a Civil Engineer of ability, a Social Philosopher of deep insight and warm affection.' He also had a fertile imagination out of which he produced, among other things, the drop- and double-ended ferryboat and a kind of submarine; then in 1798, caught by the lure of steam navigation, he drove a boat with an experimental steam engine and a four-bladed screw propeller. In 1803 he was in Europe, continuing his experiments on the Seine. Before returning to America in 1806, he saw the *Charlotte Dundas* and placed an order for a similar steam engine with Boulton and Watt of Birmingham. He also took with him a boiler made to his specification in London and these two items formed the power-unit of what became familiar to a whole

17 Colonel John Cox Stevens, 1749–1838

18 Robert Fulton, 1765–1815

generation of Americans as 'Fulton's Folly'.

This was his famous *Clermont*. Backed by Mr Livingston, a minister in the United States Government of the day, Fulton had her built in the yard of Charles Brown on the East River and named her after the residence of his patron on the Hudson River. She was decked for a short distance only at stem and stern, with the engine open to view and a house like that on a canal boat raised to cover the boiler. This house also provided accommodation for the passengers and crew. Lindsay notes with a hint of astonishment that the boilers were set in masonry. The Boulton and Watt engine, like that in the *Charlotte Dundas*, had a piston with a 4-foot stroke, but the cylinder with a diameter of 24 inches was 2 inches bigger.

Launched in the August of 1807, the *Clermont* made her historic first run from New York to Albany in the same month. The distance between the two points was 150 miles and she covered it in thirty-two

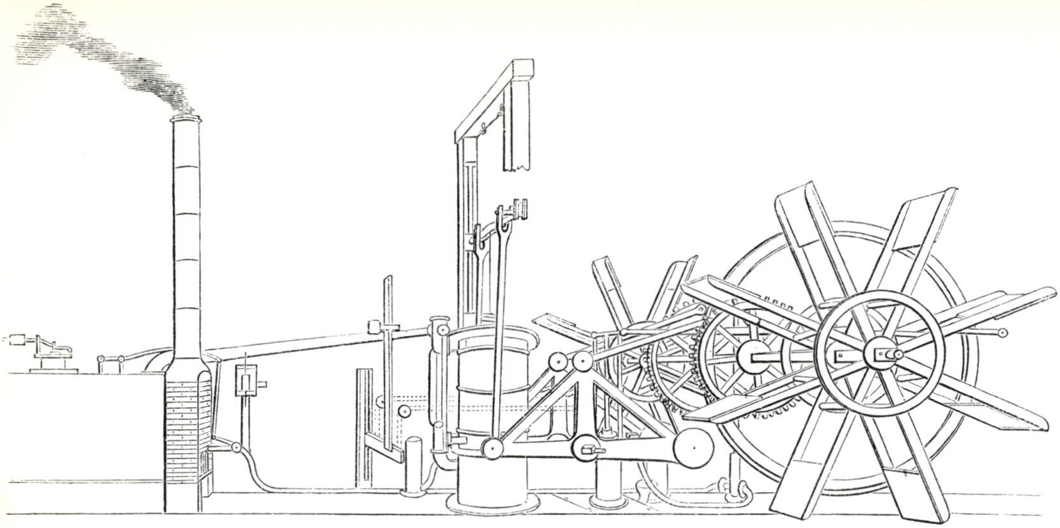

19 The power-plant of PS *Clermont*, 1807

hours out and thirty hours home, inaugurating the first-ever regular and continuous long-distance steamboat service. Fulton gives his own account of the event in the following letter addressed to the *American Citizen*:

New York, 21st August 1807

Sir, I arrived this afternoon at 4 o'clock in the steam-boat from Albany. As the success of my experiment gives me great hope that such boats may be rendered of much importance to my country, to prevent erroneous opinions, and give satisfaction to the friends of these useful improvements, you will have the goodness to publish the following facts:

I left New York on Monday, at 1 o'clock, and arrived in Clermont, the seat of Chancellor Livingston, at 1 o'clock on Tuesday; time, 24 hours, distance, 110 miles; on Wednesday I departed from the Chancellor's at 8 o'clock in the morning, and arrived at Albany at 5 in the afternoon; distance, 40 miles, time, 8 hours! The sum of this is 150 miles in 32 hours, equal near 5 miles an hour.

On Thursday, at 9 o'clock in the morning, I left Albany, and arrived at the Chancellor's at 6 in the evening. I started from there at 7, and arrived at New York on Friday, at 4 in the afternoon; time 30 hours; speed, run through, 150 miles, equal to 5 miles an hour. Throughout the whole way, going and returning, the wind was ahead no advantage could be drawn from my sails. The whole has therefore been performed by the power of the steam-engine.

I am, Sir, your most obedient,
Robert Fulton

[quoted Lindsay, iv, p. 55]

20 The *Clermont* on the Hudson, 1807

Subsequently, the *Clermont* was greatly modified. For one thing she was lengthened and decked fore and aft to provide two public rooms, 'surrounded by double ranges of berths, and fitted up for comfort in a manner then unexampled.' In her final form she was 130 feet long, and $16\frac{1}{2}$ feet beam. Her engine was rated at 18 h.p. and she is described by Lindsay as being 160 tons burden. The boiler was 20 feet long, 7 feet deep and 8 feet wide; the paddle-wheel 15 feet diameter with an axle of cast iron and paddles 4 feet long, dipping 2 feet into the water.

Fulton's second boat on the Hudson River was the *Car of Neptune* and he also built steam ferryboats to run between New York and New Jersey, a vessel to run a service through Long Island Sound and others for use on the Hudson, the Ohio and the Mississippi.

The success of the *Clermont* made him enemies, especially among those who saw her as a threat to their vested interests. Attempts were made to run the steamboat down and when this failed, political pressure was exerted to have the inventor's concession to run steamers rescinded. He was also attacked for having in effect stolen the inventions of John Fitch. This was a particularly foul lie. It is true that he developed the work of Fitch and Rumsey and borrowed from Watt, Pickard and Symington; but so did everyone else in the business and the fact does not in any way diminish his stature. He took the inventions of these men which for one reason or another had failed in their own hands and created out of them a viable entity, a thing that worked and endured.

And like the others, he got little profit from it, or so Lindsay tells us:

> . . . he himself, if reports be true, derived no advantage from it but died in 1815 very poor and almost broken-hearted through the persecution of jealous and narrow-minded rivals, leaving his family in greatly embarrassed circumstances, but at the same time leaving behind him an everlasting memorial of his energy and perseverance, and an enduring stigma on those who had taunted him with a *Fulton's Folly*.
>
> [iv, pp. 57–8]

After Fulton's *Clermont*, steam navigation became a fashionable craze and spread extremely rapidly in America. In 1809, the first steamboat was launched on the St Lawrence and the following account of her maiden voyage published in the *Quebec Mercury*, exemplifies the enthusiasm that swept the Western world for the new mode of transport and the grandiloquent terms in which the contemporary Press acclaimed it:

> On Saturday morning, at eight o'clock arrived here, from Montreal, being her first trip, the steam-boat *Accommodation*, with ten passengers. This is the first vessel of the kind that ever appeared in this harbour. She is continually crowded with visitants. She left Montreal on Wednesday, at two o'clock, so that her passage was sixty-six hours, thirty of which she was at anchor. She arrived at Three Rivers in twenty-four hours. She has at present berths for twenty passengers, which next year will be considerably augmented. No wind or tide can stop her. She has 75 feet keel, and 85 feet on deck. The price for a passage up is nine dollars, and eight down – the vessel supplying provisions. The great advantage attending a vessel so constructed is that a passage may be calculated on to a degree of certainty in point of time which cannot be the case with any vessel propelled by sails only. The steam-boat receives her impulse from an open double-spoked perpendicular wheel, on each side, without any circular band or rim. To the end of each double spoke is fixed a square board, which enters the water, and by the rotary motion of the wheel, acts like a paddle. The wheels are put and kept in motion by steam operating within the vessel. . . . [quoted Lindsay, iv, p. 58]

One must assume that the readers, like the worshippers of Hero's dancing figures, were not allowed to know how the steam operated!

Bell's *Comet*, 1812

Fulton's *Clermont* had put America a good five years ahead of developments in Europe and the man who eventually caught up with him was Henry Bell, a Scottish carpenter born at Torphichen, near Linlithgow in 1767.

Bell served his apprenticeship in a Bo'ness shipyard and worked for a time with a London engineering firm. He also studied mechanics and in 1790 settled in Helensburgh on the Firth of Clyde. Quite early in his life he became interested in the possibility of steam navigation and, first in 1801 and again in 1803, he tried to get Government backing for steamboat projects. But governments are notoriously resistant to change and what Bell was proposing implied change so far-reaching as to amount to a revolution, not only in ship design and methods of propulsion, but also in fundamental thinking. He was rejected with a snub calculated to keep him in his place thereafter and, feeling the prejudice against him at home was too strong to break down, he submitted his plans to various governments abroad. The response from the Continent was no more encouraging and across the Atlantic the United States Government merely passed his memorandum on to Robert Fulton, who wrote in acknowledgment.

Referring to this letter from Fulton, Bell subsequently wrote:

21 Bell's *Comet* on the Clyde, 1812

. . . this letter led me to think of the absurdity of writing my opinion to other countries, and not putting it into practice in my own country; and from these considerations I was roused to set on foot a steam-boat, for which I made a number of different models before I was satisfied. When I was convinced they would answer the end, I contracted with Messrs. John Wood & Co., shipbuilders of Port Glasgow, to build me a steam vessel according to my plans; 40 feet keel, and 10 ft. 6 inches beam, which I fitted up with an engine and paddles, and called her the *Comet*, because she was built and finished the year that a comet appeared in the northwest part of Scotland. [quoted Lindsay iv, pp. 63–4]

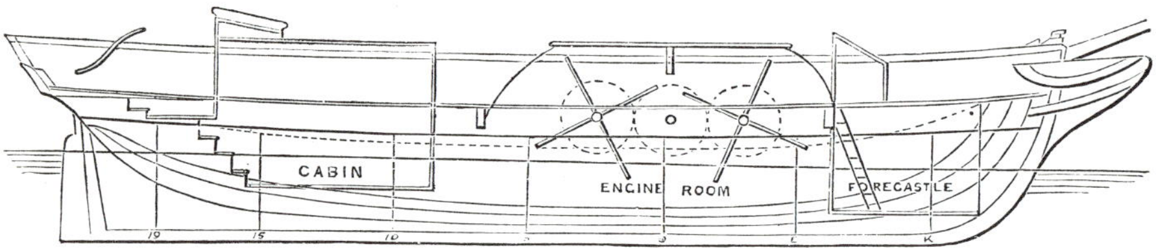

22 The engine of the *Comet* and her builder's design for the hull

Meanwhile, unlike many thwarted dreamers, Bell had continued to be diligent along other lines and prospered. By 1808, he was a successful hotelier with a hydro at Helensburgh; but the 23-mile journey from Glasgow was a great problem for his guests and it was partly in order to solve it that he had a steamboat built.

The *Comet*'s 4 h.p. engine was also designed by Bell and cost £192 to build. The vessel was launched in July 1812 and attained a speed of 5 miles per hour, becoming the first successful regular passenger steamer in Europe. The following is a contemporary advertisement of her sailings; like the announcement quoted earlier from the *Quebec Mercury*, it is redolent of the enthusiasm, the sanguine hopes and the grandiose dreams of the initiators of steam navigation:

STEAM PASSAGE BOAT

The *COMET*.

Between Glasgow, Greenock and Helensburgh,
for passengers only.

The subscriber having, at much expense, fitted up a handsome vessel to ply upon the River Clyde, between Glasgow and Greenock, to sail by the power of Wind, Air and Steam, he intends that the Vessel shall leave the Bromielaw on Tuesdays, Thursdays, and Saturdays, about midday, or at such hour thereafter as may answer from the state of the tide, and to leave Greenock on Mondays, Wednesdays, and Fridays in the morning to suit the tide.

The elegance, comfort, safety, and speed of the Vessel require only to be proved to meet the approbation of the public, and the Proprietor is determined to do everything in his power to merit public encouragement.

The terms are, for the present, fixed at 4s. for the best cabin, and 3s. the second, but beyond these rates nothing is to be allowed to servants, or any other person employed about the vessel.

The subscriber continues his establishment at Helensburgh Baths, the same as for years past, and a vessel will be in readiness to convey Passengers that intend visiting Helensburgh.

Passengers by the *Comet* will receive information of the hours of sailings, by applying to Mr. Thomas Stewart's, Bookseller Square; and at Mr. Blackly's, East Quay Head, Greenock; or at Mr. Houston's office, Bromielaw.

Henry Bell

Helensburgh Baths, 5th August 1812.

[quoted Lindsay, iv, p. 65]

The *Comet* was short on power so even 'a ripple of head wind' could reduce her to 2 miles an hour and sometimes the passengers would feel impelled to help her along by turning the fly-wheel themselves. She only drew 4 feet but as the tide ran out, it was a common experience for her to go aground about Bowling, forcing the passengers to land and walk the rest of the way to Glasgow.

In spite of all this, however, the *Comet* served her owner well until on 15 December 1820, she drove ashore at Crinan. The boat broke up but her engine was salved, and it now stands alongside Symington's of 1788 in the Science Museum at South Kensington.

But in the end Henry Bell had no joy of her. Like Fitch, Fulton and Symington, he, too, fell on hard times and was unable to pay Napier in full for the boiler. A group of public-spirited citizens interested in shipping, ultimately organized a pension for him. On this he lived out his days, dying at Helensburgh on 14 November 1830. An obelisk erected to his memory still stands at Bowling on Clydeside.

23 Matthew Boulton, 1728–1809

24 James Watt, 1736–1819

25 H. Maudslay, marine engine builder of London

3 *Innovation*

STEAM ON INLAND WATERS

WITH THE LAUNCH OF THE *Comet*, it might be said the dream had become a reality, the experiment a viable commercial proposition. The obelisk at Bowling was more than a memorial to Henry Bell and his achievement; it marked the beginning of a new phase in the development of steam navigation. There was still experimenting to be done, more and more of it as each step forward, every difficulty surmounted and problem solved, produced another challenge, but it was a different kind of man that handled it now. The visionary's day was done and his place was taken by the marine engineer, hard-headed and practical, who knew precisely what he wanted and how to set about getting it. He came to dominate the shipbuilding industry, forcing on it not one, but a whole succession of revolutions in design and construction, in methods, in the kind of materials used and above all, in the concept of what was possible.

In America the steamboat was welcomed with boundless enthusiasm. Fulton's *Clermont* had demonstrated its profitability and people fell over themselves to invest their money in it. In 1807, the same year that he built the 295-ton *Car of Neptune* for Fulton, Charles Brown of New York produced the *Raretan*, 331 tons, for service on the river of that name. Then in 1811 from the same yard, came the *Paragon*, 331 tons, engaged on the Hudson and a year later, the *Firefly* for the New York–Newburg run and the *Jersey*, 118 tons, built for the Ferry Company for their passenger service between New York City and New Jersey.

And that was only a beginning. Geographically, the United States of America was admirably suited for the development of steam navigation within her frontiers. The Great Lakes cried out for it and, operating on her enormously long rivers, the steamboat offered an easy and most profitable way of opening up vast tracts of virgin

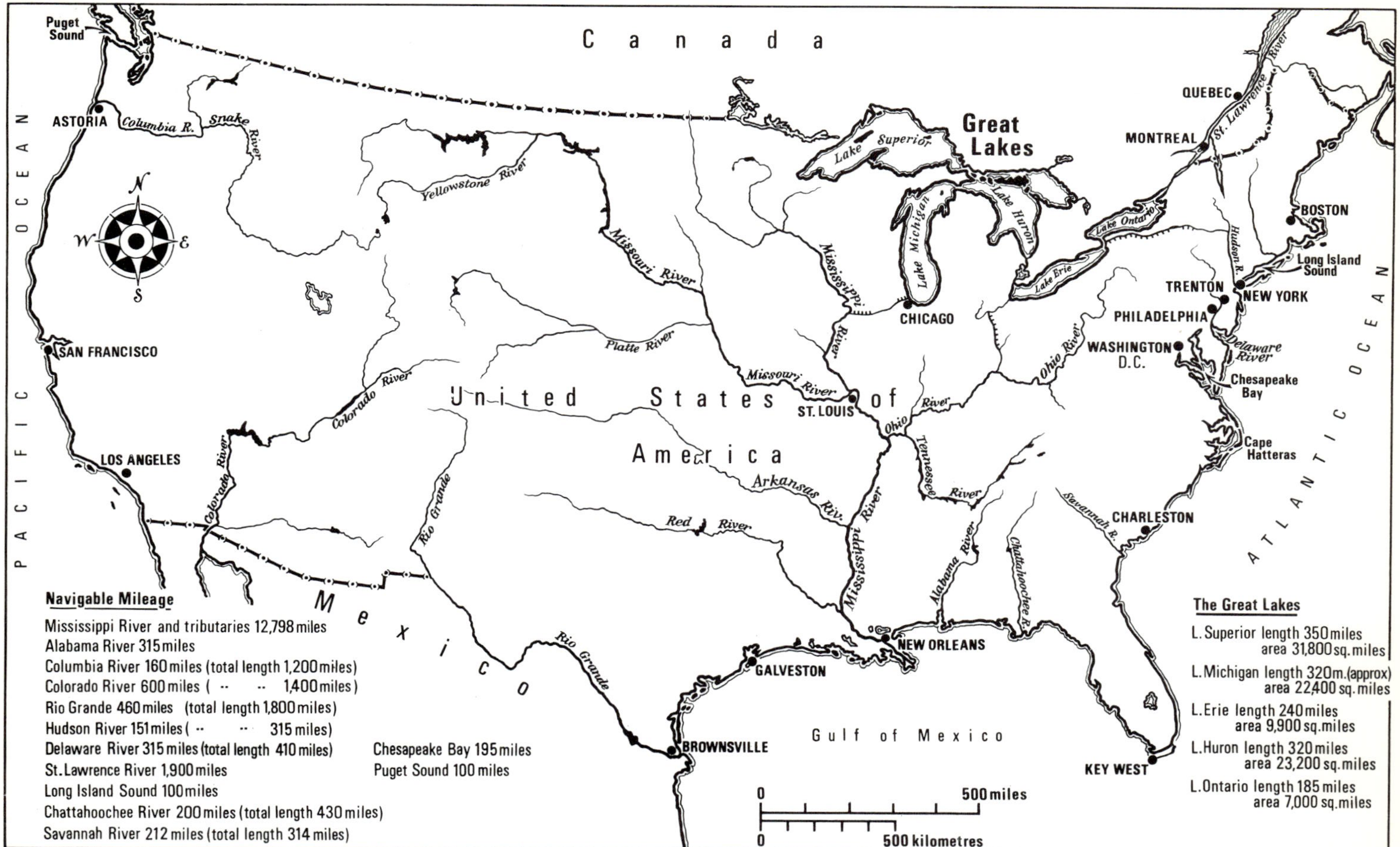

MAP No. 2 US rivers and inland waterways, showing scope for experiments

country. The Mississippi held out special promise and the first steamboat was launched on it in 1814. Lindsay omits her name but tells us that on her trial trip she ran 'a distance of 700 miles against the current', demonstrating immediately the great possibilities inherent in the new invention. America's first coastwise steamer went into service between New York and New Orleans in 1818; while the first one seen on the Great Lakes was the *Orleans* built at Pittsburg in 1811, but she was withdrawn for lack of trade and regular services were not started there until 1819. In the same year, a steamer called *Walk-in-the-Water* appeared on Lake Erie, her main customer being the American Fur Company, and by 1833 the traffic had grown so much that in that year it engaged eleven steamboats which carried an aggregate of 61,480 passengers and earned in freight just over $250,000.

The same rapid expansion was taking place elsewhere and in 1832, steamers made 900 arrivals at New Orleans from up-country, while two years after that there were 234 steamboats trading on the Mississippi and Ohio Rivers.

In the United Kingdom progress was much slower. Preble in his *Chronological History of the Origin and Development of Steam Navigation*, gives some figures that are illuminating. By 1820, he says, 100 steam vessels had been built in the United States of America and the whole of the British Empire could only boast 43, totalling 7,240 tons. This gives an average of 170 tons per ship and, as already noted, Charles Brown of New York was building them almost twice that size a decade earlier. And by 1840, the United Kingdom owned a total of 95,807 tons of steamers against 200,000 tons in the United States.

But as has been said, the early steamboats were particularly suitable and in many ways specially designed, for service on inland waterways. Thus, of that huge American total afloat in 1840, only about 4,000 tons – say 2 per cent – was registered for foreign trading. The rest was all in service on the country's rivers, lakes, estuaries and such sheltered routes as Long Island Sound. Such geographical features, comparatively speaking, hardly exist in the British Isles. A few small steamers might have found employment on the two main Scottish Firths and in the estuaries of the Severn and the Thames; but they would be no more than glorified ferryboats or competing hopelessly for freight

26 PS *Walk-in-the-Water* operating on Lake Erie, 1819

against the road transport and developing railroad systems. What Britain needed was intercontinental transport, ocean-going ships capable of making long passages and standing up to all kinds of adverse weather conditions; and the early steamers were, as yet, neither strong enough nor sufficiently powerful to fill the role.

Consequently the Admiralty at first flatly refused to consider building steamers for the Navy and, though ultimately yielding to pressure, they did so grudgingly, offering neither encouragement nor promise of reward to the designers; and long after everybody else had accepted the advantages of steam, they were still determinedly against its use in capital ships.

Fortunately, the Admiralty had no monopoly of shipbuilding and there were plenty of private citizens prepared to speculate. In 1813, a steamer was built at Leeds of all places, and started a passenger service between Norwich and Yarmouth in the August of that year. This in Lindsay's words 'was the second steam vessel launched in British waters'. The third one was built that same year in Manchester and the fourth in Bristol. In 1814, Cook of Glasgow in association with Henry Bell built two steamers, one of which – the *Glasgow*, 74 tons and 16 h.p. – '. . . became in power and efficiency the standard at that time for river steamers'; and steamboats were seen for the first time on the Humber and also on the Limehouse Canal.

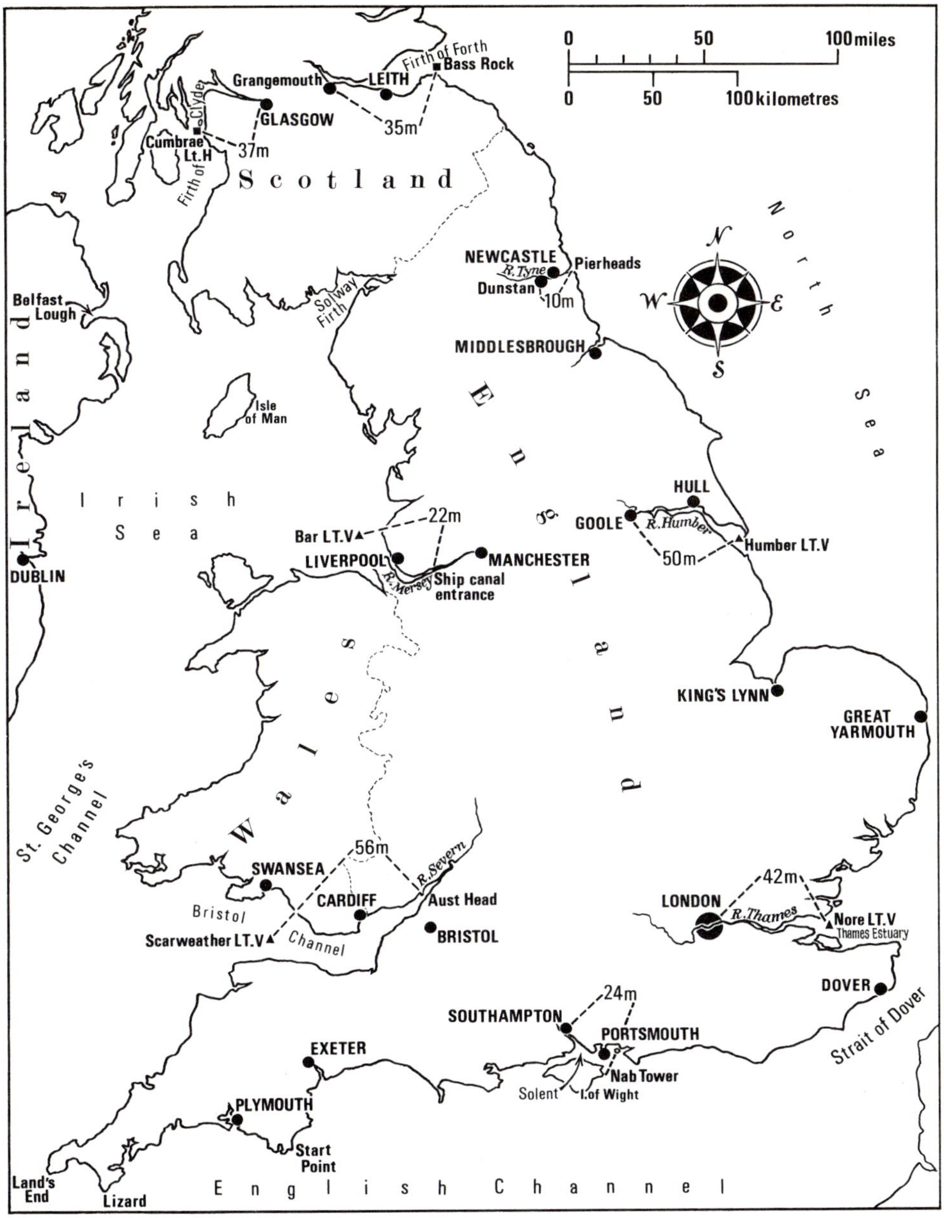

MAP No. 3 Principal British rivers and ports

Then early in 1815 another of Cook's vessels, equipped with a side-lever engine of only 14 h.p., went from the Clyde to Dublin and thence round Land's End to London. The record is silent about such fascinating details as the time she took, the speed she made and what she did about bunkers; but looking back, one can only see the voyage as an astonishing act of faith. 1815 also brought the *Morning Star*, 100 tons and 26 h.p., and the *Caledonia*, 102 tons and 32 h.p., which were launched on the Clyde; and Napier's *Marjory*, which was to inaugurate steam navigation on the Thames. That same year two Clyde-built steamers arrived on the Mersey and started carrying passengers and goods, one between Liverpool and Runcorn and the other via the canal linking Liverpool with Chester.

The following year, the *Charlotte*, a steam ferryboat plying between Liverpool and Eastham, towed the sailing ship *Harlequin* out to sea and thereby demonstrated the possibilities of the steam tug. By this time some of the prejudice had been overcome and the growing willingness of people to brave the hazard of a steamboat passage is shown in the increased number of passengers carried. '. . . in 1816', says Lindsay, 'it was not unusual for 500 or 600 passengers to enjoy, in the course of one day, water excursions on the Clyde.'

27 Channel steamer *Victory* outside Margate harbour

PS *Rob Roy*, 1818

The urge to build ocean-going steamers was not lacking among the early marine engineers. They had the vision and nobody more vividly than David Napier, who in 1818 launched the *Rob Roy* from William Denny's yard at Dumbarton. Designed for the carriage of passengers and mails, she was an immediate success in spite of being small – 90 tons burden and 30 h.p. On the Glasgow–Belfast route, she ran to time for two consecutive years without a single hitch and is notable as the first *regular* sea-going steamer in the world.

How much the Lords of Admiralty were influenced by the success of the *Rob Roy*, there is now no saying, but in 1819 the first-ever steam vessel was built for the Royal Navy. Named the *Comet*, she was 115 feet long by 21 feet beam and drew 9 feet of water. Her two engines were constructed by Boulton and Watt and rated at 40 h.p. each.

The side-lever engine

At this time, besides Boulton and Watt, only two firms – Maudslays of London and Butterley Ironworks in Derbyshire – were considered fit to be entrusted with Government contracts; but other names, now equally or even more famous, were beginning to emerge. On the Thames there were Seaward and Penn; on the Mersey, Fawcett and Forrester; and on the Clyde, Robert and David Napier, Scott, Caird and Tod. These were the men who, between them, but in the main working independently, developed James Watt's basic invention until a marine engine evolved that was predictably viable and could be built to a standard specification. This was the *side-lever engine*; and the first cross-Channel steamers, the first steam warships and the first fleets of such venerable operators as the General Steam Navigation Company and the Peninsular and Oriental SS Company were all equipped with it. It had an extremely long life for a piece of machinery. Napiers, for example, built their first one for a vessel called the *Leven* in 1823. It was rated at 33 nominal h.p. and is preserved in the grounds of Dumbarton Castle. Nearly forty years later, they were still producing them and engined the *Scotia*, last of the Cunard Company's paddlers, with side-lever engines of 4,900 indicated h.p. They had two cylinders, 100 inches in diameter and a 12-foot stroke and used steam at a pressure of 20 lb. per square inch.

Meanwhile, with techniques developing and the number of skilled craftsmen increasing, more and more coastwise steamers were being built, each one bigger and more powerful than the last and hailed as the ultimate wonder of the age. The year 1822 brought the *James Watt*, built to run between Leith and London. She was 448 tons gross and her two Boulton and Watt engines were rated at 50 h.p. each. A particularly interesting feature of her machinery was that the paddle-wheels were not coupled directly to the engines, but driven through gears. Subsequently a sister ship, the *Soho*, was built for the same trade and the assumption is that the *James Watt* was a successful development both as to size and propulsion. She was also a challenge to go one better, and in 1826 came the *United Kingdom*, built by Steele of Greenock and engined by David Napier, for the London–Edinburgh trade. Called a 'leviathan' in her day, she was 160 feet long with a beam of 26½ feet and engines of 200 h.p.

28 PS *James Watt*, 448 tons, 100 h.p. built 1822

These were all notable advances but, apart from the introduction of steamers into the cross-Channel mail services in 1821, nothing was being done to improve communications with what might be called the 'further-flung' imperial possessions. For Spain and Portugal, the Mediterranean and points beyond, letters still went by the sailing packets out of Falmouth. The only change was that at the end of the Napoleonic Wars, the Admiralty took over the running of the services from the Post Office on the grounds that the hard-driven, fast packets formed a ready-made school for seamen and a handy pool from which they could be drafted or lured into the Royal Navy as required.

Then, in 1823 the Lords of the Admiralty ordered another steamer which was described as 'representing the best practice of the day'. She was HMS *Lightning*, 126 feet long, 22½ feet wide and 296 tons. Maudslays constructed and fitted her machinery which consisted of two cylinders, 40½ inches in diameter with a 4-foot stroke and 100 nominal h.p. As a ship, she was extremely successful and remarkably durable, continuing in service just on fifty years. By the end of her

29 PS *United Kingdom*, 160 feet long, 200 h.p. built 1826

30 Side-lever engine

useful life in 1872 she had got through four sets of boilers, but her engine, of which there is a contemporary model in the National Maritime Museum at Greenwich, was unchanged.

Far-sighted business interests and frustrated Government departments continued to press for better mail services, and in 1828 Mr Hay of the Colonial Office made a formal request that a steamer be allowed to carry the mails from Malta to Corfu. The reply of Lord Melville, then First Lord of the Admiralty, is a classic example of conservative thinking. He

> . . . regretted the inability of my Lords Commissioners to comply with the request of the Colonial Department, as they felt it their bounden duty, upon national and professional grounds, to discourage, to the utmost of their ability, the employment of steam-vessels, as they considered that the introduction of steam was calculated to strike a fatal blow to the Naval Supremacy of the Empire, and to concede to the request preferred would be simply to let in the thin edge of the wedge, and would unquestionably lead to similar demands being made upon the Admiralty from other departments.

Extreme though this official view undoubtedly was, it must have reflected an opinion fairly widely held among seamen and business men directly concerned with shipping; and this conclusion is strengthened by the fact that Britain then owned approximately seventy sailing ships to every single steamer. The figures quoted by Smith are 20,000 sailing ships to 293 steam vessels. But far-sighted men still pinned their hopes on steam navigation and continued to press for improvements that only the adoption of steamers could ensure.

PS *Enterprize*, 1825

The demand for faster and more regular communications was particularly persistent from people in India and those – other than the Honourable East India Company – connected with the vast and lucrative trade with the East. Indiamen, as already noted, were desperately slow round the Cape. The believers calculated that with a steamer the passage of four to six months could be cut to something like eighty or even seventy days; and in 1822 a company was formed in London to build and run steamships in the Indian trade. A representative of the group – Lieutenant J. H. Johnston, RN – was sent out to India to drum up financial backing and promises of support and as a result of the interest and hopes he aroused, the Governor put up a proposition. He promised that 20,000 rupees (about £2,000) would be paid to any British company which, by the end of 1826, should have established a permanent service of steamers that would make two voyages out and home each year, taking not more than seventy days for the passage each way. Johnston had also raised Indian capital to a total of 80,000 rupees and it seemed that the promotion must succeed.

The next step was to acquire a suitable steamer and one was found,

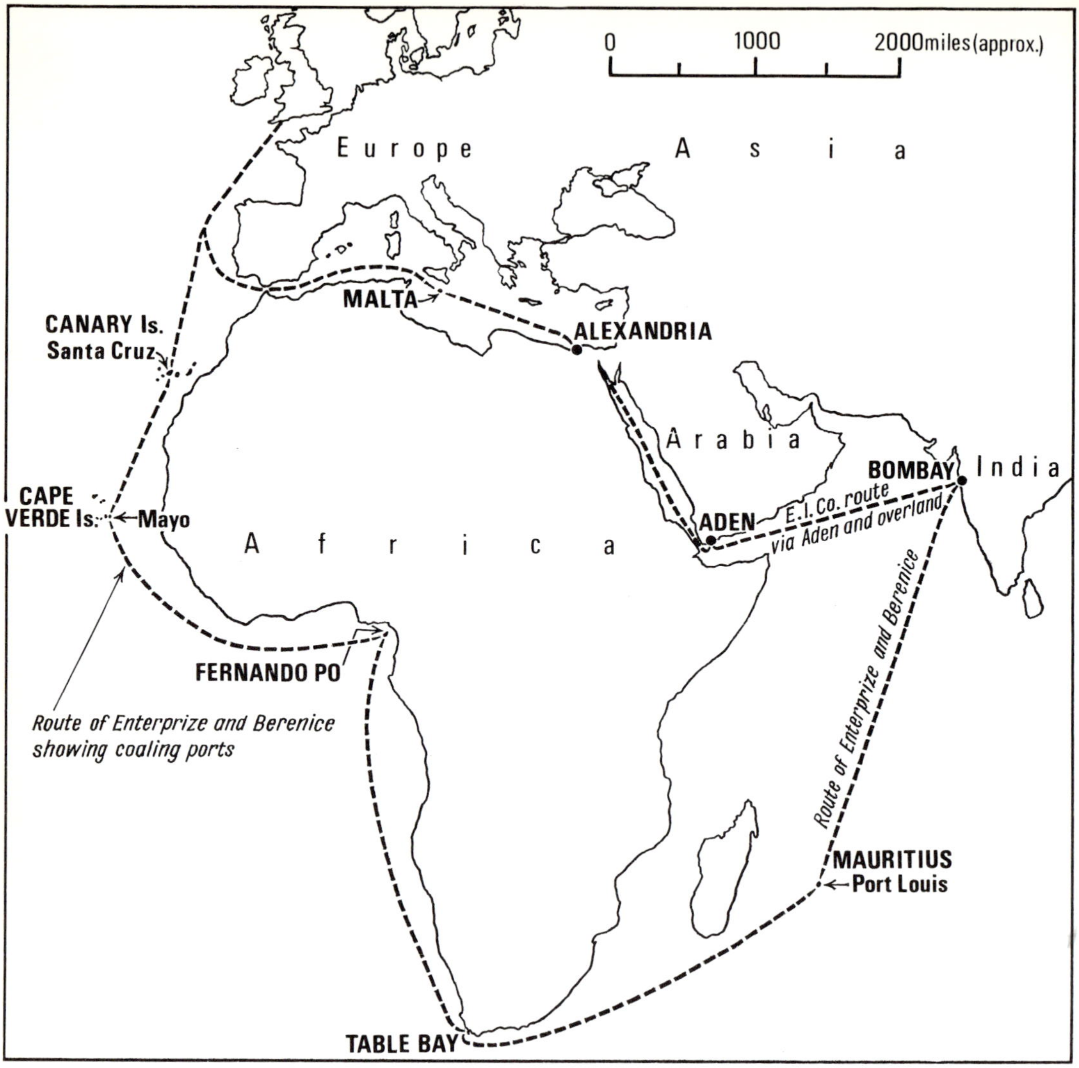

MAP No. 4 Route of *Enterprize* and *Berenice* to India, showing coaling ports

already being built in the yard of Gordon and Company of Deptford. She was the *Enterprize*, a wooden paddler of 479 tons and 120 h.p.; 120 feet long on the keel and 27 feet beam. Maudslays engined her with a two-cylinder side-lever engine, driving paddle-wheels 20 feet in diameter. The cylinders were 43 inches in diameter and the pistons had a stroke of 4 feet. With the trade winds in mind, the paddle-wheels were designed so they could be put out of gear when the ship was under sail. Another notable feature of her power-plant was the boiler. It was made in one piece and of copper. Weighing 32 tons and costing £7,000 out of the total outlay on the ship of £43,000, it was considered worth the money on the assumption that the copper would stand up to continuous service and require neither repairs nor replacement, facilities for which were not then available so far out. Other innovations were brine pumps in the engine room for discharging water from the boiler, and 'refrigerators' – so called – for heating the incoming feed-water by the outgoing brine. A large part of her bunker coal was carried in iron tanks which would be filled as the coal was burned in order to maintain the ship's trim and ensure the paddle-wheels were kept deep enough in the water.

The *Enterprize* did not live up to what was expected of her. Sailing from London on 16 August 1825 with seventeen passengers, she steamed into Calcutta on 7 December, 113 days out, killing the hopes of her owners stone dead. She was sold to the Indian Government for £40,000 and put to carrying dispatches between Calcutta and Burma.

HMS *Meteor*, 1830

By this time, more money was being made available for building and running steamships and a number of companies had been formed for the purpose. Notable among them were the City of Dublin Steam Packet Company based in Liverpool and the General Steam Navigation Company of London, which commenced operations in 1826 by sending a steamer as far as Lisbon – a singularly bold step for the time.

With the steamship continuing to demonstrate its ability to make regular and comparatively fast passages over short distances, the complaints about existing services for mails and passengers increased in bitterness and volume. The Admiralty packet ships out of Falmouth sailed once a week for Lisbon, *wind and weather permitting* and took anything up to three weeks to get there. At Lisbon, mails for Gibraltar, Malta and Egypt were trans-shipped and sent on once a month. Something had to be done and in 1830 it was decided to send letters to the Mediterranean by steamer. On 5 February 1830 HMS *Meteor*, 296 tons and 100 nominal h.p. sailed from Falmouth and inaugurated the first long-distance overseas steam mail service. The sailing packets had taken three months for the voyage to Corfu and back; the *Meteor* and her consorts *Messenger*, and *Echo*, cut the time for a round voyage to thirty-one days.

The Overland Route

The short route to India was, of course, via the Mediterranean to Egypt, then across the Isthmus of Suez and down the Red Sea and, after the fiasco of the *Enterprize*, the East India Company yielded to pressure and established what became known as the *Overland Route*. The first steamer employed on it was the *Hugh Lindsay*, 411 tons. She was built at Bombay and equipped with two 80 h.p. engines sent out from England; but her designers slipped up badly on the question of bunker capacity. The longest leg of the proposed run was the 1,710 miles between Bombay and Aden which was calculated to involve ten days' steaming – given no head winds and a smooth sea all the way – and they gave her bunker space for only five and a half.

When she left Bombay on 20 March 1829, she had bunker coal stowed, not only on deck, but everywhere else including the saloon and passenger cabins. Consequently, instead of her normal loaded draught of 11 feet 6 inches, she was down to 14 feet and her decks almost awash. Moreover, her transom was submerged and the extra load on the engines so heavy they could hardly turn the paddles round. Those who saw her sail, nicknamed her 'the Water-Lily'. Luck was with her and helped by her sails and following winds, she crawled into Aden on 31 March burning sweepings to keep her going. It took six days to bunker her at Aden and more time was lost filling up again at Mocha and Jedda. Consequently when she arrived at Suez on 22 April, she was thirty-two days sixteen hours out from Bombay, of which time no less than eleven days and ten hours had been spent in bunkering ports.

The inadequacies of the *Hugh Lindsay* and the *Enterprize* – which became her consort on the Bombay–Suez run – were not the only drawbacks to the Overland Route. Plague was endemic in Egypt and anyone coming out of the country, whether he travelled through Italy or France, had to spend a period in quarantine. Moreover, the journey itself was a considerable physical ordeal with nothing but the most primitive facilities available on the way; and the slow voyage

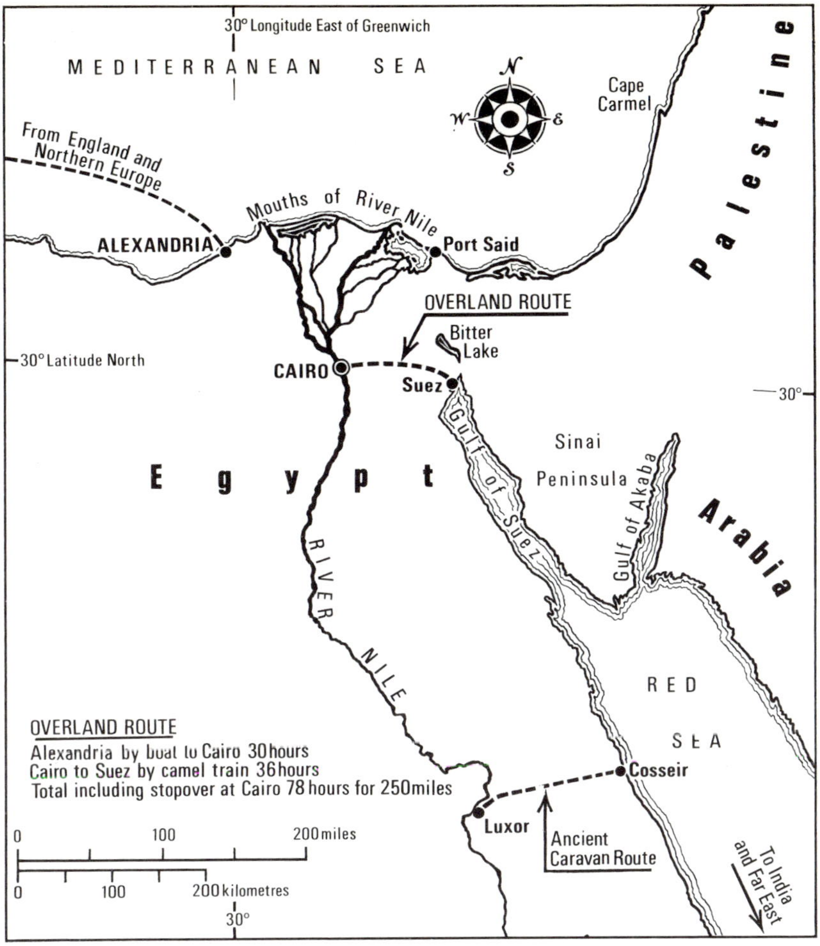

MAP No. 5 The Overland Route to India

round the Cape was very much more attractive to those who could spare the four or five months it would take. One man, however, did believe the Overland Route could be improved and speeded up. He was Lieutenant Thomas Fletcher Waghorn, RN. His particular concern was to demonstrate the time the Overland Route could save on the Indian mails if properly organized. Advised that the *Enterprize* was due at Suez on 8 December 1829, he left London on 28 October with the idea of meeting her there. His route took him across France and Switzerland to Trieste where he boarded a Spanish ship sailing

for Alexandria. Thence, he went on up the Nile by boat to Cairo, crossed the desert by camel and arrived at Suez on the day appointed.

Unfortunately the *Enterprize* had not arrived and after waiting two days, he hired a small sailing craft and pushed off down the Red Sea to find her. This he never did and putting into Jedda, he learned she was still in Bombay, laid up for engine repairs. The record is silent about his reaction to this news but it can be imagined; and after losing another month kicking his heels in Jedda, he was picked up by the sailing brig HMS *Thetis* which took him on to Bombay. In the end his journey took four months and twenty-one days; but he reckoned if the steamer had been waiting at Suez, he would have done it in fifty-five days flat.

PS *Berenice*, 1836

Waghorn had proved his point and the Honourable East India Company bestirred themselves to improve their end of the route. They put on a third steamer, the *Atlanta*. She was followed in 1836 by the *Berenice*, 640 tons and 250 nominal h.p., which Robert Napier built for the Indian Government.

Like the *Enterprize*, the *Berenice* went out round the Cape, but by then something had been done towards solving the problem of bunkers on long passages and her progress was better organized.

31 [*opposite*] The Overland Route: passengers being importuned by curio sellers aboard the P & O *Peshawar* at Aden

32 The Overland Route: stokehold of a steamship in the Red Sea

Leaving Falmouth on 16 March 1837, she arrived at Bombay on 13 June, eighty-eight days out; but out of that time she was only under steam for sixty-three days and the rest of the time was spent bunkering at various ports *en route*. Smith considers her to be Robert Napier's finest achievement up till that time and gives the following break-down of the passage:

	Distance miles	*Coal consumed tons*	*Highest speed knots*
Falmouth to Santa Cruz	1,510	128	10
Santa Cruz to Mayo	896	87	11
Mayo to Fernando Po	2,284	190	$9\frac{3}{4}$
Fernando Po to Table Bay	2,269	220	10
Table Bay to Port Louis	2,488	313	10
Port Louis to Bombay	2,612	170	10

[quoted Smith, p. 30]

Bunkers were still a problem, not only in regard to their availability but also in the intolerable amount of time lost taking them aboard in the outports; also coal consumption was extremely high, not to say prodigal, and much work was still to be done on the marine engine to increase its efficiency. Nevertheless, with that passage of the *Berenice*, the steamship was proved viable and firmly established in competition with the sailing ship on the trade routes of the world.

THE PENINSULAR AND ORIENTAL STEAM NAVIGATION COMPANY

First mail contract, 1837

Nobody ever believed more passionately in the steamship than Brodie McGhie Willcox and Arthur Anderson, shipbrokers and commission agents, who went into partnership in 1815 and opened an office in London. By 1822, they were running small sailing ships to Spanish and Portuguese ports and they introduced steamers chartered from the Dublin and London Steam Packet Company and the General Steam Navigation Company into the trade at an early date. Two of these ships – the *William Fawcett*, 206 tons and 60 h.p. and the *Royal Tar*, 308 tons and 260 h.p. – were ultimately wholly owned by them.

The firm prospered and in 1837 founded the Peninsular Steam Navigation Company, proposing to set up a regular steamer service for mails to the Iberian Peninsula. By this time they had seven ships in their fleet and were advertising them as follows:

33 Scale model of PS *William Fawcett*

Steam conveyance from London and Falmouth to Operto, Lisbone, Gibraltar, and Malaga, and vice versa, by the following new, powerful, large and splendidly fitted up Steam Ships, carrying mail from His Majesty's Post Office

Steam Ships	*Tons*	*H.p.*
Don Juan	935	300
Tagus	900	300
Braganza	650	250
Iberia	600	200
Liverpool	500	160
Manchester	600	220 (Chartered Ship)

Peninsula (Branch Steamer on the Cadiz and Seville Station)

[quoted Cable, p. 20]

It seems that although they were carrying mails, it was without a contract and they continued to petition the Government to enter into one with them. One of their methods of exerting pressure was to get items about their ships into the newspapers and Cable quotes the following as an example. It appeared on 1 June 1837.

MARCH OF STEAM: The *Iberia* steamship belonging to the Peninsular Company sailed from Falmouth on the 22nd May and arrived off Oporto on the 25th, in 66 hours. The *Braganza*, belonging to the same Company left Oporto on the 25th and arrived at Falmouth on the 28th in 70 hours, bringing letters from the *Iberia*'s passengers. So that in 136 hours or something short of six days from their leaving England, advices of their safe arrival in Portugal were back in England. [p. 32]

The mail contract was formally signed on 22 August 1837, and four days before that, the following announcement was published by the Post Office:

General Post Office
18th August, 1837

A great reduction is made in the postage upon Letters conveyed by Her Majesty's Packets in the Mediterranean. Letters for Malta, Greece, the Ionian Islands, Egypt and the East Indies, if forwarded by way of Falmouth and by Her Majesty's packets to the Mediterranean will in future, be subject to an uniform rate of only 2s. 6d. Single – 5s. Double – 7s. 6d. Treble – 10s. per ounce weight, and so on in proportion, from whatever part of the United Kingdom they may be despatched, instead of the former rates, which varied according to the distance the Letters were conveyed to Falmouth.

Single Letters for the above destinations in the Mediterranean, if specially directed 'via Marseilles' will be liable to an uniform British rate, wherever they may be posted, of 10d. and the French rate of 1s. 10½d.

in all 2s. 8½d., and Letters for the East Indies, by the same route, will be liable, in addition to those rates, the further charge of 1s. Single, and so on in proportion.

By Command,

W. L. Maberly, Secretary.

[quoted Cable, p. 33]

This first mail contract called for at least one passage a month between Falmouth and Peninsular ports as far round as Gibraltar and the subsidy to be paid was fixed at £29,600 a year. But Willcox and Anderson saw it as a beginning rather than a culmination and it might well be that even at this early date, they had their eyes on the Indian and Far Eastern trade. They certainly committed themselves to a great deal, apparently without a qualm, and publicized their undertakings widely. The advertisement announcing the new services, after listing the company's fleet and giving details of the proposed sailings, goes on:

> The first two vessels [i.e. *Don Juan* and the *Tagus*] are the largest and most powerful that have been yet put afloat. The whole of them has been fitted up so as to combine the first style of elegance with comfort to the passengers. Separate cabins for Parties and Families can be engaged.
>
> A liberal Table, with Wines, etc., is provided, and included in the Fares; and numerous unsolicited Testimonials from parties of the first rank and character, confirm the superiority of the management on board.

The announcement also explained in some detail the link-up with the naval steam packets in the Mediterranean:

> In connection with the Company's vessels, Her Majesty's Steam Ships run every alternate Week from Gibraltar to Malta, and from Malta to Corfu. Also, once a month from Malta to Alexandria, in connection with the Line of Steam communication through the Red Sea to India. Passengers for Malta, Corfu, and Greece should proceed by the Company's vessels, which leave London on the 1st, 15th and 29th September. Those for Egypt and India by the vessels of the 1st and 29th of the month. [quoted Cable, pp. 34–5]

The fares quoted were as follows:

	Chief Cabin	*Second Cabin*
London to or from Vigo, Oporto or Lisbon	£15 0 0	£9 10 0
London to or from Cadiz or Gibraltar	18 0 0	12 0 0
Falmouth to or from Vigo, Oporto, or Lisbon	13 0 0	7 0 0
Falmouth to or from Cadiz or Gibraltar	16 0 0	10 0 0

[quoted Cable, pp. 34–5]

Finally, another paragraph of historic interest gives a fair indication of the time it took to get around in those days; the details are tabulated here for clarity:

Falmouth to Vigo	54 hours
Falmouth to Lisbon	84 hours
Falmouth to Gibraltar (including 24 hours' stay at Lisbon and six hours at Cadiz)	7 days
Gibraltar to Malta	5 days (about)
Malta to Corfu	2 days
Malta to Alexandria	4 days (about)

The first ship to leave Falmouth under the new mail contract was the *Don Juan*. She sailed on 1 September 1837, made her run round the scheduled ports and leaving Gibraltar homeward bound on the 15th, ran ashore off Tarifa, 20 miles out and became a total loss. The passengers, the crew and $21,000 in specie which she was carrying were all saved and presumably the ship and cargo were covered by insurance; but the accident was a set-back and a serious blow to the new company's prestige. Nevertheless, they pressed on with their plans and somehow weathered the disaster. They not only survived, but proved conclusively that great benefit accrued to all concerned from the type of contract they had negotiated; and it is claimed that the Peninsular Company's success was the main factor in persuading the Post Office to invite tenders for the provision of a similar steamship service to the United States of America.

It also did something to the Admiralty, for in 1840 the Government sought the advice of the company on how to improve the mail service to Egypt and beyond. The result was a proposal to run the Indian mail direct by steamer from England to Alexandria, touching at Gibraltar and Malta. Tenders for this service were invited and that of Willcox and Anderson for £34,200 per annum being the lowest, was accepted. To fulfil the terms of the contract, two new ships were acquired – the *Oriental*, 1,787 tons, 420 h.p.; and the *Great Liverpool*, 1,311 tons, 464 h.p.; and by the end of that year the firm had been incorporated by Royal Charter as the Peninsular and Oriental Steam Navigation Company.

PS *Savannah*, 1819

The Atlantic had already been crossed by steamers a number of times. The first ship to do it was the *Savannah*, an American vessel built by Francis Ficket of New York. The purists claim she was no steamship but merely a sailing vessel with an auxiliary engine. Whether she was more steamer than windjammer, however, is irrelevant and what really matters is the crossing. She was 300 tons burden (some authorities say 350), square-rigged and fitted with side-paddles which could be folded rather like a fan and lifted inboard when she was running before the wind. Her engine had a cylinder 40 inches in diameter and a stroke of 5 feet. It was constructed by Stephen Vail of New Jersey. After trials on the American coast, she sailed for Liverpool on 22 May 1819, and arrived on 20 June after a passage of twenty-nine and a half days. Her log-book showed she had been under steam for a total of only eighty hours; but it was the first crossing, and there was no other until 1827.

Even at this early stage in its development, however, there were people who believed viable transatlantic services with the steamship could be established; and in 1825 a company was floated for the purpose of doing just this. The promoters had two routes in mind: one between Ireland and Nova Scotia and the other between Ireland and the ports in the West Indies. Their faith in the project is manifest in the following excerpt from a pamphlet circulated among potential investors:

> It may be assumed as an uncontravertible fact that wherever steam navigation has been established on a proper footing and on a sufficient scale of vessels and machinery, it has not only been abundantly successful, but its performance has surpassed expectations, overcome the natural prejudices and commanded the confidence of even nautical men, and it has not only drawn to it all the most valuable communications in its line of transit, but also increased it in a tenfold proportion.
>
> [quoted Smith]

The intention and the spirit behind it was admirable, but at that time ships big enough to carry the amount of bunkers required for a passage of 2,500 to 3,000 miles and powerful enough to keep to a

34 Scale model of PS *Savannah*

schedule in face of the weather conditions prevailing in the North Atlantic, were not yet in being; and the company folded up without even trying.

Other early Atlantic crossings

In 1827, the *Curaçao*, 436 tons (Kirkcaldy says 350), built at Dover the previous year and bought by the Dutch Government, made a succession of voyages from Holland to the Dutch West Indies. Steaming while the coal lasted then continuing under sail, she took about thirty days for each passage.

The next one across was HMS *Rodamanthus*, 800 tons and 200 nominal h.p., which was built by the Admiralty at Devonport in 1832. For her, a coal brig was sent on ahead, awaiting her arrival at Funchal.

35 PS *Royal William* leaving Quebec for Gravesend, 4 August 1833

The *Rodamanthus* left Plymouth on 21 April 1833, steamed across the Bay of Biscay, unshipped six floats from each paddle-wheel and continued to Madeira under sail. Bunkering from the waiting brig, she left again on 30 April and reached Barbados on 17 May. That same year, the *Royal William,* 176 feet long and about 800 tons with an engine of 200 nominal h.p. constructed by Bennet and Henderson of Montreal, crossed from west to east. Built at Quebec in 1831 to run between that port and Halifax, she was losing her owners money and they decided on the bold step of sending her to England to be sold. Leaving Quebec on 4 August 1833, with seven passengers at £20 a head, she put in at Pictou for bunkers, bunkered again at Cowes, IoW and arrived at Gravesend on 11 September. Details of the voyage are missing, but it is claimed she steamed all the way. Smith considers this doubtful in view of the length of time she was on passage. The *Royal William* ultimately went south to Bordeaux and on coming into new ownership there, her name was changed to *Ysabel Seconda.*

Junius Smith, b. 1780

At this point Junius Smith comes into the story. Smith was an American, born at Plymouth, Massachusetts in 1780. After practising successfully as a barrister in America, he went to London and began a second career, this time in business. He was a frequent traveller across the Atlantic, journeying in the fastest ships then available which were the American sailing packets. A passage to New York in August 1832 aboard the *St Leonard* cost him fifty-four days, the return to Plymouth in the *Westminster* another thirty-two days and finding the waste of time intolerable, he turned his mind to the idea of transatlantic steamships and was moved to write:

> Thirty-two days from New York to Plymouth is no trifle; any ordinary sea-going steamer would have run it with the weather we had in 15 days with ease. I shall not relinquish the project unless I find it absolutely impracticable. [quoted Smith]

Ignoring alike the forebodings of his friends, the ridicule of the unbelievers and the opposition of those whose interests his success might jeopardize, he floated a company which was registered in 1835 as the British and American Steam Navigation Company. The following year, he wrote to New York:

> I have the pleasure to inform you that the directors of the British and American Steam Navigation Company have contracted for the building of the largest and intended to be the most splendid steamship ever built, especially for the New York and London trade, she will measure 1,700 tons, 200 feet keel, 40 feet beam, three decks, and everything in proportion. She will carry two engines of 225 horse-power each, 76 inch cylinder, and nine feet stroke. The expense of this steam frigate is estimated at £60,000. These large undertakings will require time to mature, but I think the business will at last be done effectually.
> [quoted Smith]

The ship was no pipe dream. First called the *Victoria* and then the *British Queen*, she was built by Curling and Young of Limehouse, who had just delivered the *Iberia* to the Peninsular Steam Navigation Company. Her engines were constructed by Girdwood of Glasgow.

Brunel's PS *Great Western*

Junius Smith was right; his undertaking took time to mature and while it was doing so, others were taking a hand, notably in Bristol where the Great Western Steamship Company was formed and in Liverpool in the shape of the Transatlantic Steamship Company. The Bristol firm, which numbered among its active members Isambard Kingdom Brunel (1806–59), beat all the rest and produced the first steamship specially designed and built for the Atlantic trade.

She was the *Great Western*, 1,320 tons, 400–750 h.p., built by Patterson and engined by Maudslays to Brunel's design. In size and power she was a considerable step forward, being 236 feet long and 35¼ feet in the beam. Her engines had cylinders 73½ inches in diameter with a stroke of 7 feet.

Meanwhile Girdwood, building the engines for the *British Queen*, had failed to keep the delivery date, but Junius Smith would not be thwarted and to keep faith with his backers, he chartered the *Sirius*, 703 tons and 320 h.p., from the St George Steam Packet Company and dispatched her to New York on 28 March 1838. This marked the beginning of what, for the steamship, might well be called the *annus mirabilis* (miracle year).

The *Sirius* was designed for the home trade. She was 208 feet long, 25 feet beam, built by Menzies and engined by Wingate. Her cylinders were 60 inches in diameter and the stroke 6 feet. She was equipped with the surface condenser invented by Samuel Hall in 1834 which enabled fresh distilled water to be used for boiler-feed and obviated the tedious, time-wasting business of periodically clearing the boilers of salt.

Calling at Cork to bunker and pick up mails, she sailed again on 4 April at 10 a.m. carrying a total of forty passengers – eleven cabin, eight forward cabin and twenty-one steerage. For fuel she had 450 tons of coal, 58 casks of resin and for the boilers 20 tons of fresh water. Bonsor says 'she was dangerously low in the water' and the passage must have been a considerable ordeal for all on board; but she survived and arrived in New York on 23 April, eighteen and a half days out from Cork.

The *Great Western* left Bristol with only seven passengers aboard, four days after the *Sirius* sailed from Cork and arrived at New York on the same day as the smaller ship, only a few hours later.

36 PS *Sirius*, 703 tons, 320 h.p. 1838

37 PS *Great Western*, arriving New York 23 April

Accounts of these two pioneer passages differ in detail, but there is a strong impression that the voyage of the *Sirius* was a rather desperate affair. In the modern idiom, they played it by ear, with a lot of do-or-die improvisation. In the *Great Western* however, nothing was left to chance; every eventuality was foreseen and provided for while she was still on the drawing-board and she couldn't lose. Enormous strength was built into her as the following quotation from the Field MS. shows:

> Her scantling is equal in size to that of our line of battleships, it is filled in solid, caulked within and without up to the first futtock heads before planking, and all above this height is of English oak. The flooring is of immense length, each floor overrunning the other, they are strongly dowelled and bolted in pairs first and also together by 1½ inch bars of 24 feet in length, driven in parallel rows, scarfing about four feet. She is trussed in the firmest and closest manner by iron and wooden diagonals and also shelf pieces, these, including all her upper works, are fastened with screws and nuts to an immense extent. [quoted Smith]

Maudslays built the engines to match. They weighed 200 tons and were bolted to 'a vast frame, the beams of which extend to and press equally on every part of her bottom'. Her four flue boilers were 11½ feet long, 9½ feet wide and 16½ feet high, with the flues above the furnaces.

On that maiden passage, she covered 3,125 nautical miles at an average speed of 8·6 knots (Smith gives her slightly more than this: 215 miles a day against Kirkcaldy's 208) on a consumption of 43 tons of coal a day; and the subsequent history of the two ships shows the better performance of the *Great Western* was no fluke and owed nothing to the vagaries of the weather.

As for the *Sirius*, she left New York on her maiden eastbound passage on 1 May and crossed in sixteen days; then after one more round trip which lost money, she was taken off the run and the company suspended operations for a year. The *Great Western* however, went on from strength to strength. On her first eastbound crossing, she carried sixty-eight passengers and 20,000 letters, upped her average day's run by 5 miles, reduced her consumption to 28 tons a day or 393 tons for the passage and made it in fourteen days. On the second voyage she carried sixty-five passengers out and ninety-two home, and finally completed five round trips in 1838. She remained on the North Atlantic until 1846 by which time she had made thirty-seven round voyages – seventy-four crossings. Her overall average passage was fifteen and a half days westbound and thirteen and a half days eastbound and her best ever, was twelve days and seven hours from New York to Bristol in 1842. She was acquired by the Royal Mail Steam Packet Company in 1847 and scrapped ten years later. Her quality is shown by the report of the Lloyd's surveyor who inspected her in dry dock after she had steamed a total of 75,000 miles. He found her 'to be in perfectly good condition, free from any indication of defect inside; the copper smooth and without any apparent strain outside' (quoted Smith).

Two other ships, both out of Liverpool, entered the Atlantic trade that year. The first of them, like the *Sirius*, was chartered to fill a gap. She was the *Royal William*, 617 tons – not to be confused with the Quebec-built vessel of the same name – owned by the Dublin Steam Packet Company and hired from them by the Transatlantic Steamship Company while a steamer they had bought on the stocks was being completed. Only 175 feet long, 27 feet in the beam with engines of 270 h.p. constructed by Fawcett and Preston, the *Royal William* was much too small for the trade. Nevertheless, on her first passage westward, she demonstrated conclusively the superiority of the steamer over the sailing ship. Leaving Liverpool on 5 July 1838, she overhauled the *Hibernia* which had left the same port eighteen days before her, and also passed the *Sir James Kempt* which was then no less than fifty-eight days out from Dundee, to arrive in New York on the 24th, but after two more round voyages she was withdrawn and returned to her owners.

Meanwhile the *Liverpool*, 1,150 tons, which she had temporarily replaced, came into service. Built by Humble and Milcrest and engined by Forrester, she was the biggest steamer constructed on the Mersey to date, her dimensions being: length 223 feet; breadth 30 feet 6 inches; cylinders 75 inches diameter; stroke 7 feet; horse-power 468. She sailed from Liverpool on 22 October and, being driven back to Cork by stress of weather, did not arrive in New York until 23 November; but her actual passage time was only sixteen and a half days. Her best day's run was 242 miles and her worst 151 miles; but the bad luck of her maiden voyage seems to have clung to her and though she made six round voyages in 1839, the last of them was a very poor performance. Homeward bound, she was driven

south all the way to the Azores, whence, after rebunkering, she finally arrived home, twenty-seven days out. Shortly after this in 1840 the Transatlantic Steamship Company was wound up and the *Liverpool* sold off to the Peninsular and Oriental Steam Navigation Company.

PS *British Queen*, 1839

The *British Queen*, 1,863 tons, that brain-child of Junius Smith, sailed from London on her maiden voyage on 11 July 1839, calling at Portsmouth and making her departure from there at noon on the 12th. Aboard her were 220 passengers, including Mr Smith, 600 tons of bunker coal, some mails and about 80 tons of cargo. A contemporary writer described her as 'a most beautiful specimen of London ship-building, and for elegance of mould, great strength and admirable proportion of parts, thought by many to be unequalled'. Without the journalistic extravagance, she was 245 feet long and 40½ feet beam. Her engines, built in the end by Robert Napier, had cylinders 77½ inches diameter with a 7-foot stroke and were rated at 500 h.p. Although there was little difference between her time for the outward passage on her maiden voyage and that of the *Great Western*, over a period of time Brunel's creation proved not only faster but more reliable; and in 1841 after a passage of twenty-four days during which she was severely knocked about, the *British Queen* was withdrawn and sold to a Belgian company.

But by then, regular scheduled sailings both ways across the Atlantic were well established; the Royal Mail Steam Packet Company was running a twice-monthly service to the West Indies and the Pacific Steam Navigation Company was covering the west coast of South America. The period of innovation was over and in the words of Sir John Rennie '. . . there seemed no bounds to the extension of steam navigation.'

38 [*opposite*] PS *Liverpool*, 1,150 tons, 468 h.p. on her maiden voyage to New York, October 1838

39 [*opposite*] PS *British Queen*, 1,863 tons, 500 h.p. 11 July 1839

4 *Wooden Hulls and Paddle-wheels*

DEVELOPMENTS IN THE USA

ALL THE EARLY STEAMERS had wooden hulls with paddle-wheels for propulsion. Such ships, as already noted, operated on the Atlantic and in the Pacific, on Indian Ocean routes and along the shores of the Mediterranean; but it was on the rivers, lakes and inland waterways of the United States of America that this form of steam navigation, initiated by Fulton's *Clermont*, was most successful and reached its ultimate in magnificence.

PS *Chancellor Livingston*, 1816

Fulton built his last and biggest in 1816. She was the *Chancellor Livingston*, 526 tons, 157 feet long, 33·5 feet beam, with a service speed of 6·5 miles an hour, and said to have cost upwards of £25,000. She was a side-wheeler with the paddles set precisely amidships, engine and boiler both being on the foreside of them. Several novel features were incorporated in her design. For example, the paddle-wheels were boxed in to prevent splashing and a deck built out over the sponson beams provided space which was used for stowage and also for latrines. The area immediately round the engine was mainly taken up with wood and coal-bunkers (she was the first American steamboat to burn coal), but also accommodated the galleys and refreshment bar. There was a casing over the engine boiler, but it was open at the sides for ventilation. The wheel-house, giving an uninterrupted view forward, was erected on the engine casing.

Except for the captain and the purser who had cabins on the main deck next the baggage-room, the crew lived in the forecastle and the passenger accommodation was divided into two classes. Forward was the second-class cabin with four two-tiered rows of curtained berths – one on either side and two back-to-back down the middle. The after end was reserved for first-class passengers. It provided a large dining-saloon with two-tiered berths along the sides but none in the middle; the upper berths each had a side-light and there was a ladies' cabin on the deck above, reached by a companion-way aft.

Lindsay makes no mention of this one, but he had a great admiration for the American paddle-steamers and the men who built them. Looking back from 1875, he wrote:

> More conversant at this period than any other nation with the most approved style of ship-building and possessing an abundant supply of materials at a comparatively low price, they were able when steam vessels were first introduced, to construct them at a lower cost than any other people; and if they had not the same facilities for obtaining steam engines, these could easily be obtained from England. [iv, p. 130]

He is enthusiastic about the special fineness of line in their hulls, and the size and power of their engines as well as the 'immense diameter of their paddle-wheels'. Some of them had connecting-rods 19 feet long and a stroke of 10 or 11 feet. They also worked much faster than the English counterparts; 'the piston passing through the space of

40 The saloon of an American steamboat

41 Mississippi river boats racing by moonlight

500 feet in a minute', all of which led to great economy in fuel, and much higher service speeds. But Lindsay reserves his greatest praise for the adventurous spirit of the American engineers. They were not content, it seems, with the strictly limiting and totally predictable low-pressure steam currently used in English engines. On American ships, even the low-pressure condensing engines were worked at 10–30 lb. per square inch; and for those using expansion alone, steam was generated at anything from 50 to 150 lb. Although safety valves were fitted, it was common practice to circumvent them in various ways, often enough with catastrophic consequences. Lindsay notes:

> Between 1816 and 1848, no less than 233 steamboats employed on American waters exploded, some of them involving terrible disasters, the lowest number during that period being one annually, but sometimes there were as many as ten, twelve, and thirteen in the course of a year. The loss of life in each accident averaged eleven persons, being a total of 2,563 human beings killed, besides 2,097 persons wounded. In one terrible explosion, that of the *Louisiana*, on the New Orleans levee, nearly 200 persons lost their lives. [fn. iv, p. 140]

PS *New World, c.* 1850

The speeds attained by these craft in the middle of the nineteenth century are almost unbelievable. On the run between New York and Boston by the East River and Long Island Sound, they were covering the 140 miles in seven and a half hours including one stop on the way and 20 miles an hour seems to have been fairly common. But even this was bettered by the steamboats running on the Hudson River, which appear to have reached their peak of perfection in the *New World*:

> This graceful and magnificent vessel is 380 feet in length. Her breadth of beam is 50 feet, or 85 feet over all, including the sponsons and paddle-boxes, while the diameter of her paddle-wheel is no less than 45 feet and that of her cylinder 76 inches, the length of stroke being 15 feet. The *New World* has 347 state rooms or cabins and 600 sleeping berths. . . . Although the *New World* was one of the largest and most magnificent vessels employed on the Hudson, she was surpassed in speed by the *Daniel Drew*, which has attained the extraordinary rate of 25 statute miles an hour without assistance from either wind or tide. . . .
>
> [Lindsay, iv, p. 150]

42 Boiler explosion aboard PS *Isaac Newton en route* from New York to Albany, 1864

Again it must be stressed that these were essentially river craft. The demands made on them were all limited and foreseeable. The passages they traversed were short and the routes they covered invariably sheltered. With the possible exception of those on the Great Lakes, they were not subjected to the constant pounding and straining of running seas and long ocean swells; and never being more than an hour or two away from a supply of fuel, they needed relatively little bunker space. Consequently they could be designed on the finest of lines and lightly built with the minimum of hull in the water and the lavishly decorated and furnished passenger accommodation piled up fore and aft on the main deck.

THE FIRST CASUALTIES

For long deep-water passages and intercontinental trades, the designers and builders of both hull and engine faced a completely different set of problems. Enormous strength had to be built into the wooden hulls, not only to stand up to the battering of the sea but also to carry the very great weight of the engines without falling apart under the strain. Then the engines themselves had to be made stronger and the ratio of their power to the gross tonnage higher. And finally an inordinate amount of available space on board, already reduced by the great size of the engine, had to be allocated to bunkers. The fate of Junius Smith's British and American Steam Navigation Company illustrates these difficulties most vividly.

PS *President*, 1839

While the *British Queen* was making her maiden voyage in the summer of 1839, her consort was already building in the Limehouse yard of Curling and Young; and the company was widely advertising their intention to build more ships so sailings could be maintained on the 1st and 16th of each month. The new ship, launched in the December, was named the *President*. She was the biggest yet – 243 feet long, 41 feet beam and 2,366 gross tons. Engined by Fawcett and Preston of Liverpool, she had cylinders 80 inches in diameter, a stroke of 7 feet 6 inches and was rated at 540 h.p. She was well built with heavy oak timbers stiffened fore and aft with iron, and contemporary reports

43 PS *President*, 2,366 tons, 540 h.p. 1839

described her as 'presenting a very handsome appearance to the superficial beholder', though the old salts were critical of her lines and could not see her breaking any records.

The *President* was unlucky from the start and was almost lost in the English Channel while being towed to Liverpool for her engines to be fitted. Leaving Liverpool on 1 August 1840, she took sixteen and a half days to New York, thus proving herself slower than both the *British Queen* and the *Great Western*. She made one more round voyage that year and left Liverpool for her third on 10 February 1841, arriving in New York on 3 March – a disappointing passage of twenty-one days. Sailing again for Liverpool on 11 March, she was sighted off Nantucket Shoal at four o'clock the next afternoon by the sailing ship *Orpheus* whose master reported she was 'labouring heavily and shipping much water'. She was never seen again and stands in the records as the first steamer to be lost on the Atlantic ferry run.

Following the disaster, the owners took a long, cool look at the situation then issued a statement which showed the profit earned by the *British Queen* averaged £1,256 per round voyage, the corresponding figure for the *President* being £1,350; but this was gross profit, and when depreciation, insurance and management expenses had been deducted, the conclusion was reached that as things were '. . . it was virtually impossible for any North Atlantic steamship line to continue in existence without a subsidy.' That subsidy had already been granted to another firm, so the cold logic of the accounts was accepted and with the sale of the *British Queen*, the British and American Steam Navigation Company went out of business.

Passage times, 1838–9

Leaving the question of economic viability aside, however, there was no doubt about transatlantic steam navigation being worthwhile and the following table shows the superiority of even the first steamers over sail. It is compiled from information published in the *Shipping Gazette* and the *Civil Engineer's Journal* for 1840 and compares the performance of the first three steamers with that of the best of the sailing packets, from the maiden voyage of the *Great Western* on 8 April 1838 to the arrival home of the *Liverpool* on 11 January 1840:

	Longest outward (*days*)	(*hrs*)	*Shortest outward* (*days*)	(*hrs*)	*Average outward* (*days*)	(*hrs*)	*Longest home* (*days*)	(*hrs*)	*Shortest home* (*days*)	(*hrs*)	*Average home* (*days*)	(*hrs*)
SAILING SHIPS												
Old or Black Ball Line	48	—	22	—	33	17	36	—	18	—	22	12
Dramatic Line	38	—	23	—	30	12	25	—	17	—	20	12
Star Line	45	—	27	—	36	—	28	—	21	—	24	—
Swallowtail Line	45	—	28	—	35	—	31	—	17	—	22	12
STEAMSHIPS												
Great Western	21	12	13	—	16	12	15	—	12	6	13	9
British Queen	20	9	14	21	17	8	21	12	13	12	16	12
Liverpool	18	12	16	—	17	4	27	—	13	18	15	16

[quoted Smith, p. 48]

Thus over a period of some twenty months a saving is shown of approximately seventeen days on each outward voyage and seven days on each homeward and what is perhaps more important, the gap between the longest and shortest passages is greatly reduced, demonstrating the potential regularity and greater reliability of the steamship.

EARLY RIVALRIES

Samuel Cunard, 1787–1865

The man with the Government subsidy was Samuel Cunard, son of a Philadelphia merchant and born at Halifax, Nova Scotia in 1787. It is said that he had the idea of establishing a service of steamers for passengers and mails across the Atlantic several years before the *Great Western* proved it a practical proposition; and in 1838 he came to England for the purpose of seeing what could be done about it. His starting-point was the Secretary of the Honourable East India Company with whom he was acquainted. This man gave him an introduction to Robert Napier of Glasgow who in turn put him in touch with George Burns of the same city and David MacIver of Liverpool. Burns and MacIver agreed to back him financially if he could obtain a contract for the carriage of mails, and Napier was to build the ships.

In October 1838, the Admiralty, satisfied at last that steamers would be faster, safer and more reliably regular than sailing ships on the North Atlantic, advertised for tenders for the carriage of mails to North America. It was confidently expected that the Bristol Company whose *Great Western* had proved the route and been so outstandingly successful, would get the contract; but Cunard's tender, besides calling for a lower subsidy, offered other advantages which the Admiralty could not very well refuse, and he got the prize. As a consequence, in 1839 Cunard, Burns and MacIver formed the British and North American Royal Mail Steam Packet Company to run between Liverpool and Halifax, Boston and Quebec, and Robert Napier started building.

The contract called for two voyages a month during eight months of the year and one a month during the remaining four. The subsidy was originally fixed at £55,000 per annum, but raised to £81,000 when it became clear that four steamers instead of three would be

44 Samuel Cunard, 1787–1865

needed to maintain the service. Cunard had in mind ships of about 800 tons and 300 nominal h.p., but Napier thought this was too small for the North Atlantic and on his advice four larger and more powerful steamers were built.

PS *Britannia*, 1840

These first Cunarders were the *Acadia*, *Britannia*, *Caledonia* and *Colombia*. The *Britannia*, 1,156 tons and 207 feet long, was the biggest but only by 20 gross tons and a foot in length. They were, of course, wooden ships propelled by paddle-wheels and, as was still the custom, they carried some sail, being rigged as three-masted schooners with square topsails on the foremast. The engines, built by Robert Napier were of 740 indicated h.p. with two cylinders 72½ inches in diameter and a stroke of 6 feet 10 inches. At 16 revolutions per minute they drove the ship at 8½ knots and consumed between 31 and 38 tons of coal per day. The new company's mail service was initiated by the *Britannia*. Leaving Liverpool on 4 July 1840, she arrived at Halifax twelve days and ten hours later, averaging 8½ knots.

Napier's carefully designed and extremely well-built steamers were an immediate success, and before very long the owners of the American clippers began to feel the effects of competition in a field where they had enjoyed a virtual monopoly and absolute supremacy. Reluctant to abandon the fast sailing packets, they came up with the idea of getting the best of both worlds by fitting them with auxiliary engines. This way, it was argued, they would keep pace with the steamers in head winds by using the engines, and outstrip them by many knots when the wind was in their favour. So in 1845, the clipper ship *Massachusetts*, 751 tons with accommodation in her long poop for thirty-five first-class passengers, was fitted with a steam engine and a screw propeller. She was owned by R. B. Forbes of Boston who on 15 September 1845 dispatched her from New York to Liverpool, where she arrived on 3 October, eighteen days out. After two round voyages, the *Massachusetts* was sold to the United States Government and the project abandoned.

The Ocean Steam Navigation Co. (USA)

And now national prestige became a factor in the development of steam navigation on the North Atlantic. In October 1845, the United States Postmaster-General advertised for tenders for the carriage of mails between America and Europe in competition with Cunard; and the owners of the fast sailing packets, at last reading the writing on the wall, responded. No fewer than six tenders were submitted and as a result the Ocean Steam Navigation Company came into being the following year. The firm had a nominal capital of $1,000,000 and a subsidy of $400,000 a year for a fortnightly service between New York and Bremen, calling at Southampton. Operations began with two wooden paddle-steamers, the *Washington* and the *Hermann*, both of 1,650 tons. The *Washington* took the first sailing in June 1847, leaving Boston for Southampton on the same day as the *Britannia* sailed from New York for Liverpool. The result was in effect the first international steamship race across the Atlantic; but, although the *Washington* was the more powerful ship, she was no match for the first Cunarder which made port two whole days before her.

The next challenge came from France, when in 1847 the Transatlantic General Steam Packet Company of Le Havre was floated with a subsidy of £15,000 and a loan of £15,000 as working capital from the French Government. This one was still-born, lost £80,000 and went broke within a year without ever owning a bottom.

PS *United States*

Then the owners of the famous Black Ball Line became involved and produced the first full-powered American steamer to run on the New York–Liverpool route, i.e. in direct competition with the Cunarders. She was the *United States*, 1,900 tons, a wooden paddle-steamer which made one round voyage to Liverpool, followed by four on the New York–Southampton–Le Havre run, after which she was sold to the North German Navy and ultimately destroyed by fire in 1862.

The Collins Line, 1847–58

Among the tenders submitted to the United States Government in 1845 was one from E. K. Collins, founder of the Dramatic Line of sailing packets. He asked for a subsidy of $385,000 a year for ten years, during which time he undertook to maintain a fortnightly service of steamers between New York and Liverpool for eight months and a monthly service during the remaining four months of each year. This proposition did not come before Congress until June 1846 and was turned down; but nine months later it was resurrected and passed 'after a brief debate'. How much the continuing success of the Cunarders influenced this decision, there is no saying, but it must have been a factor.

So the New York and Liverpool United States Mail Steamship Company, generally known as the Collins Line, and the most important of the early American-owned companies on the North Atlantic came into being. It was a prestige operation from start to finish. The plan was for five steamers and they had to be the biggest, fastest and most lavishly equipped ever built, for the avowed purpose was 'to run the Cunard off the service'. Consequently design after design was discarded in favour of a more ambitious one and all the

45 The Collins liner *Pacific*, 3,000 tons, 800 h.p. 1850

time the costs were rising until in order to keep the project alive, the Government had to increase the proposed subsidy and advance $25,000 of it on each ship each month until it was launched.

In the end only four steamers were built instead of five. They were the *Atlantic*, the *Pacific*, the *Arctic* and the *Baltic*, all of 3,000 tons – two and a half times the size of the first Cunarders – with engines of 800 h.p. Massive strength was built into them, the frames being of oak, stiffened by much ironwork and the planking of pitch-pine. Lessons learned from the *Britannia* and her consorts were freely used and the result was a quartet of wonderful ships but at a ruinous cost. The same extravagance went into their interiors, which were over-ornate even by present-day standards. They had steam heating in the cabins, bathrooms and a barber's shop, and originally all the 200 berths were first class, though after a year in operation the accommodation was extended to include 80 second class.

The first sailing of the new line was taken by the *Atlantic* on 27 April 1850, which was a whole year later than originally planned. She didn't have much luck either, getting herself involved with some pack ice and damaging her paddle-floats. Consequently her first

46 Typical steamship lounge of the 1850s

passage was thirteen days, but her sister ships did better and soon beat the best the Cunarders could manage. By 1852 the *Arctic* had marked up a passage of nine days seventeen and a half hours from New York to Liverpool, an average of 13·21 knots. These results, however, were achieved at a prodigious price, not only in running expenses but also in abnormal wear and tear on the engines which were maintained only by big squads of mechanics working night and day while the ships were in port. In 1851 the company carried 50 per cent more passengers out and in to Liverpool than the Cunarders, but were still losing money hand over fist. The following year Congress agreed to increase the subsidy to $858,000 per annum until December 1854, after which it would be subject to withdrawal on six months' notice.

Cunard expands

Meanwhile Cunard and his partners had not been idle by any means. A fifth ship, the *Hibernia*, had been added to the fleet and by 1847, they were the only British firm left operating on the route. In that year the original mail contract expired and a new one was made. This called for a weekly service during eight months of the year and a fortnightly one for the remainder and upped the subsidy to £156,000 per annum. To meet the new commitments, four new steamers were built at a cost of £80,000 each, and the first of them, the *America*, 1,800 tons, made her maiden voyage in April 1848. In 1850, when the threat of the Collins Line became a fact instead of a projected bogy, building was started on two more ships, in addition to the *Asia*, 2,200 tons and the *Africa*, 2,200 tons, then completing. But the fleet was still considered inadequate and at the end of 1851 the *Arabia*, 2,400 tons, was added. This one, the last of the wooden Cunarders, matched the Collins liners for luxury of accommodation, and among the amenities she provided were steam heating, two libraries, a smoking-room and a cupola over the dining-saloon to give it more height. Bonsor reckons she was the least successful of the big wooden paddlers.

PS *Persia*, 1854

Up till this time the Government had insisted that all ships carrying mails should be of wood, though Cunard were already using iron ships on other services; but when this restriction was removed in 1854, Robert Napier built for them the iron-hulled paddle-steamer *Persia*, 3,600 tons, which marked the beginning of a new phase in the struggle for supremacy on the North Atlantic route. The *Persia* was 390 feet long, 45 feet wide with engines of 4,000 indicated h.p. She was designed and built to take back the speed record from the Collins Line, an exercise which in fact proved to be unnecessary, other factors resolving the conflict.

Disasters of the 1850s

Although they were already in deep water financially, the Collins Line continued to plan on a large scale. A major disaster was added to their troubles, when on 27 September 1854, the *Arctic* westbound out of Liverpool collided with the French steamer *Vesta* in foggy weather off Newfoundland. She sank with the loss of 322 lives, among them the owner's wife and two children. A replacement was laid down and while she was building, the service continued with the remaining three. Then on 23 January 1856 came the second misfortune. The

Pacific, with 45 passengers and a crew of 141, sailed from Liverpool and was never heard of again. Kirkcaldy thinks she foundered after colliding with an iceberg – 'a victim, perhaps to the insane desire for speed, which then as now, was one of the unfortunate features of Trans-Atlantic voyages'.

End of the Collins Line, 1858

The new ship ordered after the loss of the *Arctic* was launched in the April of 1856 and scheduled to sail on her maiden voyage from New York in the following October; but delivery was delayed while watertight bulkheads were fitted and Collins had to charter in order to fulfil the terms of his contract. In the event, the new ship – the *Adriatic* 3,700 tons – did not sail until November 1857 but she fulfilled her promise with a passage of ten days seven hours. She had cost the company £250,000 and along with this enormous bill came six months' notice from Congress that the subsidy was being slashed to $385,000 a year – less than half the current figure of $858,000. It was decided that there was no possible hope of carrying on and at the end of the *Baltic*'s westbound voyage in February 1858, the company ceased to operate. Kirkcaldy's epitaph, though tart, is probably fair enough comment. He wrote:

47 PS *Persia*, 3,600 tons, 4,000 i.h.p. 1854.
Section through engine-room.
Note side-lever engines

> The history of the Collins Line emphasises the fact that in order to compete successfully and at the same time avoid financial loss, a steamship company required, in addition to fine ships and powerful engines, good business management. Both here and later in connection with the *Great Eastern*, the work of the engineer and ship-builder ended in failure through business ineptitude. [p. 63]

Nevertheless, by his efforts to go one better than Cunard, Collins contributed significantly to the development of steam navigation. The competition was a tremendous stimulus to designers of both hulls and engines and resulted in rapid advances in size and power, as well as great improvements in services; and, what was perhaps more important in the end, it challenged the virtual monopoly of Cunard and forced them to reduce their charge of £7. 10*s.* a ton on freight by nearly 50 per cent.

PS *Scotia*, 1862

There was nothing inept about the management of the Cunarders. Cunard was determined to have the fastest ship on the North Atlantic run and although the big paddle-steamer was expensive to build and even more so to run, it was still the fastest thing afloat. Consequently he went on building them, covering the extra costs by expanding into other services maintained by economically viable units. His last paddler was the *Scotia*, built in 1862. She was 379 feet long and her side-lever engines gave her a speed of 14 knots on a consumption of 160 tons a day. With accommodation for 275 first-class passengers and stowage for just over 1,000 tons of cargo, she was extravagant and obsolete but she was also extremely popular.

Pacific Mail Steamship Company (USA), 1847

Another American firm in wooden paddlers was the Pacific Mail Steamship Company. Like the Collins Line it was floated in 1847 and it, too, had a Government subsidy – amount unknown – but there the resemblance ceased, for the Pacific Company was a success from the start. Committed to serve the still undeveloped Pacific coast, there were great difficulties to overcome before it could get started. Workshops and repair yards had to be set up at Panama, San Francisco and Astoria, a dry dock constructed and coal depots established all along the route. Of all these items coal was the biggest problem, for it had to be carried round the Horn in sailing ships, either from the eastern seaboard of the United States or from England and cost anything from $20 to $50 a ton. But it was done and the company's first steamer, the *California*, left New York on 6 October 1848 to become the first to carry the United States flag into the Pacific. She was followed in quick succession by the *Panama*, the *Oregon*, the *Tennessee*, the *Golden Gate* and the *Columbia*. They were just in time to meet the enormous demand for transportation created by the discovery of gold in California and established a regular service between Panama and San Francisco, maintaining the extraordinary average speed of 254 miles a day including stops at various ports on the way.

The Pacific Mail Company went on building wooden paddle-steamers long after the iron hull and screw propeller had made them obsolete, yet Lindsay is extremely enthusiastic about the enterprise and pioneering spirit of the firm, which quickly reached out to cover not only the Pacific coast of North America but also the West Indies, Mexico, Central and South America. By the 1860s their ships were crossing the Pacific to China and Japan and, writing in 1875, Lindsay describes the company as 'by far the greatest of the American maritime undertakings'. By then they owned thirty-three steamers with a total cargo capacity of 74,000 tons and were making regular calls at fifty ports – three on the Atlantic coast and forty-seven in the Pacific.

PS *Great Republic*, 1867

The China run was started in 1867 with four of the biggest wooden paddle-steamers ever built – the *Great Republic*, *China*, *Japan* and *America*. They were about 4,000 tons gross and fitted with 'walking beam' engines which drove them from San Francisco to Yokohama in twenty-two days, and thence to Hong Kong in seven days more. With these and the rest of their fleet the company set up a network of services bewildering in its scope and complexity. Lindsay describes it as follows:

> The steamers engaged on the China line leave San Francisco for Yokohama and Hong Kong every alternate Saturday, connecting at Yokohama with their branch steamers for Shanghai and at Hong Kong with the English and French steamers for Singapore and the principal ports in India, and via the Suez Canal, with the Mediterranean and Atlantic

48 Negro women coaling an RMSP Company's steamer at Kingston, Jamaica

ports of Europe. The New York and Panama Line connects at Aspinwall with the Royal Mail Steam Packet Company to Southampton; with the West India and Pacific Steam Packet Company to Liverpool; with the Hamburg–American Steam Packet Company to Hamburg, and with the Compagnie Générale Trans-Atlantique to France. At Panama they connect with the Pacific Steam Navigation Company to all South American ports. The Mexican and Central American line leaves San Francisco every alternate Thursday for Panama, stopping at all Mexican and Central American ports. The New York and Panama line leaves New York every alternate Saturday and San Francisco every alternate Wednesday. [iv, p. 155]

This wonderful success story offset the failure of the Collins Line; but in the end, the Pacific Company, like the Cunard, abandoned the wooden paddler and went in for the iron hull and screw propeller, for such was the price of survival.

The Royal Mail Steam Packet Company, 1841

Another company which stuck to wood and paddle-wheel until the late 1860s was the British Royal Mail Steam Packet Company. Formed in 1841 to carry the mails between England, the West Indies and the Gulf of Mexico, this undertaking planned on a big scale from the start. Under the terms of their contract with the Admiralty, their ships had to be 'substantial and efficient in all respects, and of such strength that would enable them to carry guns of the largest calibre then in use on board Her Majesty's war-steamers, with engines of not less than 400 collective horse-power' (Lindsay, iv, p. 293); and they began by building no less than fourteen of them. The subsidy, £240,000 per annum for ten years, was on a scale to match their thinking, but to earn it they had to cover a lot of ground. The original terms called for services totalling 684,816 miles a year, but when the company showed a loss on the first year's working of £79,790. 16*s.* 8*d.*, the Government agreed to reduce the mileage to 392,976 instead of raising the subsidy to a more appropriate figure.

The *Forth* 1,900 tons gross, 450 nominal h.p. was the largest of the company's original fleet; and these ships were the finest in every respect that the builders of the day could produce. She was built by Menzies of Leith and no expense was spared in fitting her out, elegance and convenience being the overriding considerations in the accommodation just as strength and efficiency were in the hull and machinery.

In spite of all the portents, the big thinking and the lavish expenditure, in spite of being engaged on fine-weather routes devoid of such hazards as fog, ice and mountainous seas, the RMSP Co. made a disastrous start, losing seven of their ships in ten years. The *Isis* was the first to go, sinking off Bermuda on 8 October 1842 after striking a reef. The second one was the *Solway* which on 15 April 1843 foundered 20 miles west of Corunna with the loss of sixty lives; and the third was the *Medina*, which tore her bottom out on a coral reef off Turks Island on 12 May 1844. Then came the *Tweed*, 1,800 tons and 450 h.p. Bound for Vera Cruz across the Gulf of Mexico, she ran up on the Alicranes Reef off the Yucatan Peninsula on 12 February 1847 and became a total loss. Of the 151 people aboard, passengers and crew, 72 were drowned and the remainder suffered terribly before they

49 Launch of the *Forth* at Leith in 1841

50 Loss of the *Amazon* by fire in 1851

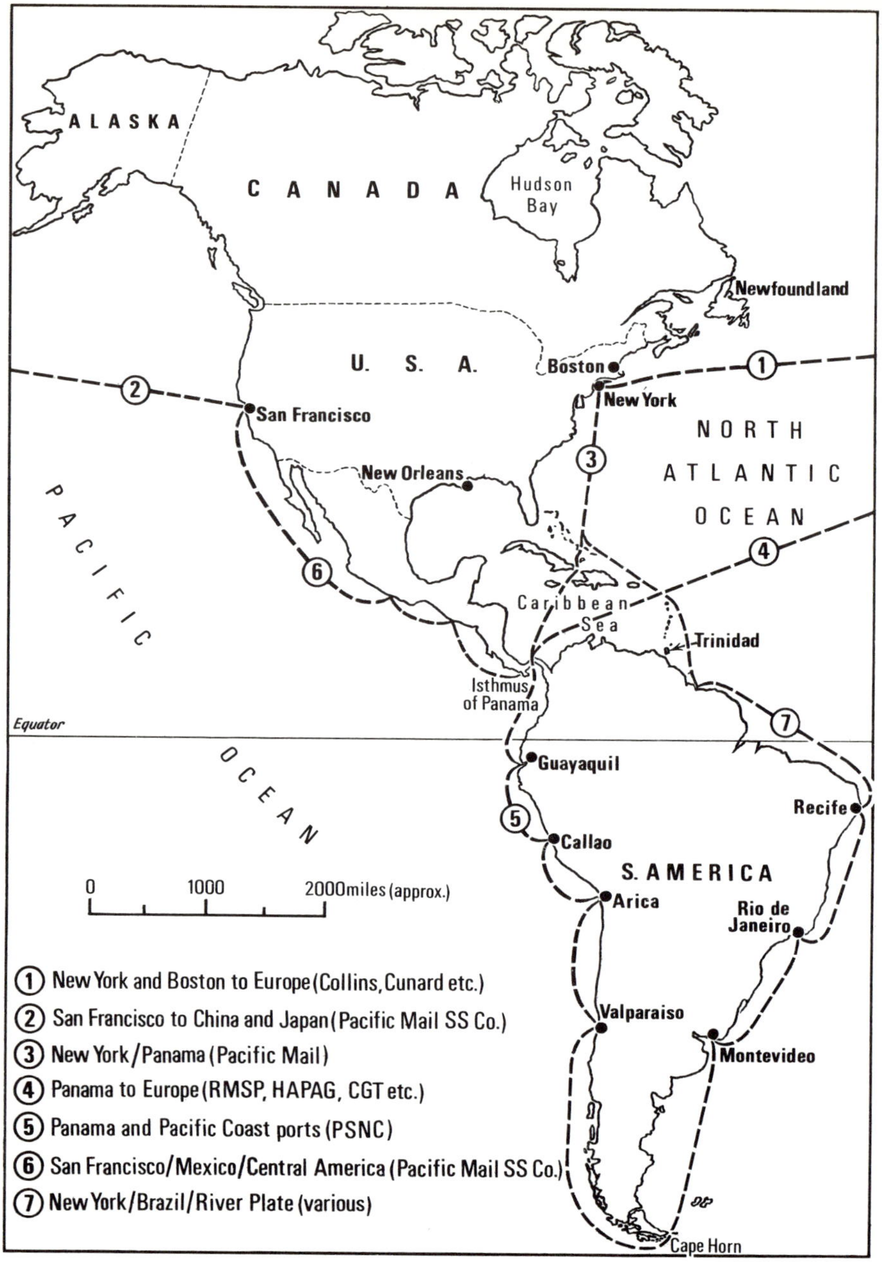

MAP No. 6 Trade routes round the Americas *c.* 1860, showing connections with Europe

were rescued. Two years later almost to the day, the *Forth* struck the same reef and she too was a total loss. The following year, the *Actaeon*, betrayed by a faulty chart, stranded on a shoal outside Cartagena, and never got off. Finally and probably worst of all, came the *Amazon* disaster.

At the time of her launch from the Blackwall yard of R. & H. Green on 28 June 1851, the *Amazon*, 2,256 tons register, 800 h.p., was the biggest wooden merchant steamship ever built. She was 300 feet long, 41 feet beam and 32 feet deep. Her engines, constructed by Seaward and Capel of Millwall, had cylinders 96 inches in diameter and a stroke of 9 feet, and normally drove her 41-foot-diameter paddle-wheels at 14 revolutions per minute. On trials, loaded down to 19 feet forward and 19 feet 9 inches aft, she logged 11 knots. Designed for long passages, she had bunker space for 1,000 tons of coal – enough to keep her going for sixteen and a half days at her normal consumption of 2½ tons per hour in twenty-six furnaces. Ready for sea, she represented a capital outlay of £100,000.

Sailing on her maiden voyage with a total of 160 people on board, she caught fire 110 miles west-south-west of the Scilly Isles and was completely destroyed. Only 46 of those who sailed in her survived.

Despite this succession of grievous losses, the company prospered and the trade on the routes they covered increased so rapidly that in 1843, even after allowing for the two ships lost, the accounts showed a gross profit of £94,210. Nor was this any mere flash in the pan, for the following year, the surplus was £147,749 and by 1851 the financial position was so strong, that the directors were able to advance £25,480 towards the completion of the railway across the Isthmus of Panama. By this time, of course, the California gold-rush was well under way with all its consequent expansion of trade and it looked as if the established lines could never again show a loss.

The mail contract was renewed for a further ten years from the beginning of 1852, with the subsidy increased to £270,000 per annum on condition that the company should inaugurate and maintain a monthly service 'to the Brazils'. This increased the mileage to 547,296 and in effect reduced the rate of remuneration from 12*s.* 3*d.* to 9*s.* 10*d.* per mile. But it still paid and the company added five new steamers to their fleet – wooden paddlers of 2,250 tons gross and 800 h.p. Lindsay reckons that after making allowance for what was received in postage, the RMSP services were costing the country about £180,460 per annum.

In 1857, the company was called on to reduce the time taken by mails from England out to Rio de Janeiro and back again, from sixty-six days twenty-two hours to fifty-five days nineteen hours. The directors were also asked to provide three more ships of 3,000 tons and 800 h.p. for the West Indies service and a fourth, somewhat smaller, to make better time between Rio de Janeiro and the River Plate. The immediate result of this programme was the reduction in the time taken by the mail between England and the Isthmus of Panama from fifty-nine days to forty-two, with three days overlap at the homeward end.

This kept them going and prospering until 1868, when the contract again came up for renewal. By then, even the Lords of Admiralty were prepared to admit the wooden paddle-steamer was out of date and as Lindsay puts it, they

> . . . relieved the company from the condition of building wooden vessels adapted for purposes of war, and the directors themselves discovered that iron was preferable to wood and the screw a better mode of propulsion than the paddle-wheel. . . . [iv, p. 311]

whereafter they turned to John Elder and Company of Glasgow for an entirely different kind of ship.

Arthur Anderson's belief

The P & O unlike the RMSP Company, were using iron ships at a relatively early date, and in 1842 they built the iron-hulled PS *Pacha*, 592 tons, 210 h.p. It was the same with the screw propeller, introduced into their fleet by the *Shanghai*, 546 tons, 100 h.p. in 1851. But these were tentative essays. The last wooden ship in the fleet was the PS *Vectis*, 841 tons, 1,058 indicated h.p., built in 1853 and the last iron paddler, the *Nyanza*, 2,082 tons, 2,304 indicated h.p., which came in 1864. Thus it would seem that the company tried to have the best of both worlds, but it would be quite wrong to assume from this that they were backward-looking and lacked enterprise. The fact is, that of all the pioneer steamship owners who survived the first quarter century of deep-water steam navigation, the P & O was probably the most adventurous and forward-looking.

Arthur Anderson, who was one of the founders of the firm and its managing director from 1837 to 1868, based all his thinking on a passionate belief *that trade follows the facilities for it.* Consequently he was prepared to initiate and run a service at a loss, in the confident expectation that regular and fast communications would attract more traffic and eventually turn the loss into continuing and expanding profit. Having undertaken the carriage of mails between England and Egypt, he argued that an increased flow of traffic between India and Egypt would enhance the volume of trade on the company's new route. With this in mind when the firm was granted its Royal Charter in 1840, he gave an undertaking

> . . . that within two years, the P. & O. would establish a mail service with suitable steamers between India and Egypt; and this undertaking was given without any contract or offer of payment for the service except that the East India Company promised an annual payment of £20,000 if they made four voyages in the first year, six in the second year, and one a month in the next three years. [Cable, p. 44]

To achieve this was a stupendous task. In the first place, it entailed designing and building an entirely new type of steamer, one bigger and more powerful than any hitherto operating in Eastern waters. This essentially experimental ship had to be got out to India via the Cape, by a route on which there was no provision for bunkers and supplies of food and fresh water were at best problematic and at worst unobtainable.

And getting there was only the beginning of the story. The East India Company with all its vast resources had tried for years to establish a regular service of steamers between Bombay and Suez, but the best they could manage was one trip a year. Anderson was proposing to start from scratch with Calcutta as the base, and this meant setting up not only a large bunker depot there, but also stores, workshops and administrative offices. Indeed the only item that caused no headaches was manning, for Anderson seemed to attract to his service the best men available and made it worth their while to stay, as the following pay scale of 1839 shows:

	£	*s.*	*d.*	
Captain	20	0	0	per month
Mate	7	0	0	
Second Mate	4	0	0	

Chief Engineer	12	0	0
2nd Engineer	8	0	0
Firemen	3	5	0
Quartermasters	3	0	0
Seamen	2	10	0
Carpenter	5	0	0
Cook	3	0	0

[Cable, p. 44]

Not exactly princely, maybe, but it compared favourably with the going rate and had the additional advantage of being steady – a rare thing in the hungry 1840s.

PS *Hindostan*, 1842

The ship was ordered and while she was building, agents were sent out under sail to establish and stock the necessary service stations along the route she would follow. Launched in 1842, the new steamer was named *Hindostan*. She incorporated a number of new developments and marked a significant step forward in design. Her tonnage was 2,017 and her side-lever engines, constructed by Fawcett were rated at 520 indicated h.p. Although built of wood, she had numerous iron bulkheads and a special fire-extinguishing installation, both facts calculated to inspire confidence in her strength and safety. The accommodation provided for passengers was also well ahead of contemporary standards, for of the 150 berths available aboard her, 20 were in single-berth cabins; and no expense was spared on the furniture and fittings which were in a single word, luxurious. Finally the directors, convinced that absolute reliability was more important than economy, had opted for flue boilers instead of the less voracious tubular ones, a decision which blandly accepted a consumption of 6½ lb. of coal per indicated horsepower, per hour.

Probably they felt justified in spreading themselves a little in view of the results shown in the First Annual Report, issued in November 1841. This showed the company had eight steamers – two of them 1,600-tonners – at sea and another two 1,600-tonners building and declared a final dividend of 3½ per cent, making 7 per cent for the year. In view of what was happening to other companies in the business, they might be forgiven for concluding that their results were 'unprecedented in the lot of any steam undertaking at so early a stage in its proceedings' (Cable, p. 73).

51 PS *Hindostan*, 2,017 tons, 520 i.h.p. leaving Southampton 24 September 1842

The *Hindostan* got away from Southampton on 24 September 1842 to a send-off like a Royal fleet review – ships dressed overall, yards manned and bands playing as she steamed past. Some of her passenger accommodation had been reserved for a party boarding at Cape Town, but there was intense competition for the rest and she sailed with a full list. Cable estimates they paid £40 a head for the trip, inclusive of wines and spirits, a total of £6,250, which went a long way towards covering the cost of getting her out to India. The passage took ninety-one days, but twenty-eight of them were spent in ports of call replenishing the bunkers. Her stops were at Gibraltar, St Vincent, Cape Verde Islands, Ascension, Cape Town, Mauritius and Point de Galle, Ceylon.

The directors, with supreme confidence in her success, signed a new mail contract that same month, and in return for a subsidy of £115,000 a year undertook to run a regular service between Calcutta and Suez with calls at Madras and Ceylon.

The *Bentinck*, 1,974 tons, but otherwise identical with the *Hindostan*, went out to Calcutta in 1843; she was followed in 1844 by the

Precursor, 1,817 tons, 500 h.p., and with her arrival the Calcutta–Suez service was fully established. The last of the trio was nowhere near so grand as the other two. She was bought on the stocks and though she did nearly 11½ statute miles per hour on her trials, she had limitations otherwise, being able to stow only 200 tons of cargo with 550 tons of bunkers.

Improvements on the Overland Route

52 The Overland Route. View of Mahmoudieh Canal

While all these matters were progressing, the company took a long cool look at the famous Overland Route across the Isthmus of Suez and decided something had to be done about it.

The Overland Route, as Lieutenant Waghorn had demonstrated, was the shortest way from India and the Far East into the Mediterranean basin and the great trading centres of northern Europe. It was also the oldest and had been in use since the beginning of recorded history. Till the advent of the steamship, Oriental merchants shipped their goods and supercargoes in dhows across the Indian Ocean and up the Red Sea. Prevailing winds made Suex virtually inaccessible to this kind of craft and they usually put in at Cosseir, about 250 miles south of that port. Thence the goods were transported across the desert by donkey and camel-train to the Nile near Luxor, to be loaded into boats again and floated down river via Cairo and Alexandria to the Mediterranean. The route we have described above had been improved to some extent by the cutting of a canal linking Afteh on the left bank of the river, with Alexandria; but the journey was still a daunting experience and undertaken only under pressure of extreme urgency.

The P & O eased the strain a little by putting a steamer on the Nile between Luxor and Afteh. This reduced the river transit to something like twenty-four hours, but the desert journey remained and with the forty-eight miles of the Mahmoudieh Canal to traverse in a horse-drawn boat, Cosseir to Cairo still took five days out of a man's life – always assuming he didn't die of cholera or be eaten alive by the bugs, fleas and infinite variety of other savage vermin on the way. Then a second steamer, the *Cairo*, a remarkable vessel carrying up to 100 passengers and doing 15 miles an hour but drawing only 2 feet of water, was sent out; and after some difficulty with Waghorn, the company took over the whole enterprise – desert transit and rest-houses included. They even built their own hotel in Cairo and reserved it exclusively for their passengers.

By this time, the Overland Route had been robbed of most of its terrors and quite a lot of its discomforts. It had also been speeded up, the official schedule for the outward journey being:

Alexandria to the Nile	12 *Hrs*
Nile to Cairo	18
Stop-over in Cairo	12
Cairo to Suez	36
Total for 250 miles including stops	78

The effect of the improvements on the volume of passenger traffic was immediate and marked, the totals carried being:

1838/1839	Average: 125 per year each way
1841:	Under P. & O. 573
1842:	Under P. & O. 800

Thereafter the annual totals of passengers and goods rose rapidly until anything up to 4,000 camels would be employed on the desert transit of one single ship's loading. The cargoes of course, were high-cost commodities such as silk, indigo, spices and specie, which alone could absorb the expense of this kind of handling.

Extension to China, 1844

Still operating on Arthur Anderson's dictum that trade follows the establishment of facilities for it, the P & O in 1844 contracted for the extension of the Indian mail service from Ceylon to Penang, Singapore and China. The China mail was to be transhipped at Point de Galle monthly, the schedule being:

Ceylon to Penang	140 *Hrs*
Penang to Singapore	45
Singapore to Hong Kong	170

The *Lady Mary Wood*, 553 tons, 250 h.p., a wooden paddler built in 1842, was sent out round the Cape to initiate the new service and landed the first mails at Singapore on 4 August 1845, just forty-one days after they left London via the Overland Route.

In 1852 the P & O was given a new contract under which they were to provide:

1 A bi-monthly line between England and Calcutta.
2 A monthly mail between Bombay, Ceylon and China.
3 A monthly mail between Calcutta and China.
4 A new service between Singapore and Australia connecting at Singapore with the English mails.

But still the East India Company hung on to the Bombay–Suez route and flatly refused to give it up to the P & O. It was costing about £100,000 a year to run and was hopelessly inefficient and unreliable. The issue was hotly debated in Parliament, one member informing the House, presumably out of his own experience, that 'the East India Company's ships could carry only a few passengers and little merchandise; or indeed had barely room for the passengers' luggage'. But the East India Company went on defying criticism, until one day there just happened to be no steamer available to carry the mail and the bags were put aboard a sailing dhow. This was an intolerable step backwards, yet they would probably have got away with it, if it had not been for the fact that the dhow never reached Suez and all the mail was lost.

That was the end of the road for the Honourable East India Company and the Bombay–Suez service was at last entrusted to the P & O.

SS *Himalaya*, 1853

In 1853, to meet these enormous and constantly expanding commitments, the company built no fewer than eleven new ships. Two of them – the *Valetta*, 832 tons, 1,027 i.h.p. and the *Vectis*, 841 tons, 1,058 i.h.p. – were wooden paddlers; one, the *Tartar*, 303 tons, 557 i.h.p., an iron paddler; and another, the *Himalaya*, 3,508 tons, 2,050 i.h.p. was laid down as a paddler. She was the biggest steamer in the world, 340 feet long, 44 feet beam and 35 feet deep, the ultimate in ship design, with accommodation for 200 first-class passengers, of whom 170 could be fed at one sitting in her 100-foot-long saloon; but while she was building the directors read the writing on the wall. They petitioned the Admiralty for permission to convert her to screw propulsion before she was launched, and as ten long and eventful years had elapsed since Brunel's *Great Britain* had been floated out of dry dock to be fitted with a screw propeller, it was hardly a revolutionary idea. The Lords of the Admiralty reluctantly agreed to the request.

The company had done very well out of the paddle-wheel. Before its services to India were established, British trade with the East was put at about £20 million a year, but by 1868 it had risen to £110 million and virtually the whole of the steamer traffic with Eastern ports was in the hands of the P & O at this time. The volume of trade across the Isthmus by the Overland Route alone was running at £40 million a year. The paddle-steamers had started it all and proved beyond any question the truth of Arthur Anderson's dictum that *trade follows the facilities for it*.

But as the nineteenth century moved into its third quarter, the P & O, in common with all other far-sighted shipowners, began to phase out their wooden paddle-steamers and replace them with iron ships, screw propelled. The day of the ocean-going paddle-steamer was done, but it had played a wonderful part in opening up the world and knitting its peoples together.

5 *Iron Hulls and Screw Propellers*

THE FIRST BUILDERS IN IRON

IF IT COULD BE SAID that the world owed iron steamships to any one man, it would not be Isambard Kingdom Brunel, although he built the biggest, the most famous and the longest lasting of them all, but Henry Cort, the ironmaster who in 1783 invented *puddling* – a method of processing iron that purified it to the point where it was fit to be rolled into plates and bars. This discovery was the prerequisite for the development of railways, bridges and boilers. It gave the mechanical engineer the malleable, reliable material he needed for his art and the early iron ships were the product of that art and not the work of the orthodox shipbuilder.

The iron hull: pros and cons

Like the visionaries who first dreamed of steam navigation, the men who proposed to build ships of iron, met not only scepticism, but actual hostility and obstruction, particularly from the Admiralty and other Government agencies. To begin with it was difficult to persuade people that an iron vessel would float. Another objection was that if the thing did not sink under its own weight, the engine would make it sag and break its back. Then some, who should have known better, suggested that an iron ship sailing with the sun on one side for any length of time would gradually heat up on that side and expand, subjecting the whole structure to disastrous stresses and strains. Finally there was the question of corrosion, which it was maintained nothing on earth could prevent. Years after the iron hull had proved successful, the chief constructor at one of the Royal Navy dockyards could still say in all seriousness, '. . . don't talk to me about ships of iron; it's contrary to nature.'

The official objection of the Lords of the Admiralty was that a shot fired through iron plates fragmented badly. In consequence, iron was declared an unsuitable material for the building of men-of-war and its use was also banned for merchant ships engaged in the transport of mails, since these were to be part of the fighting force in time of need.

These arguments were, of course, pure nonsense, but there were two very real difficulties to be overcome before iron could entirely replace wood as a material for building ships. The first of these was the effect of the metal on the ship's compasses, and this was eventually overcome by building compensating devices into the binnacle; the second defect was the proneness of the iron hull to become foul with marine growths when submerged in salt water so the longer the voyage, the more serious the fouling and consequent loss of speed. This, though never completely overcome, was brought under control by the development of anti-fouling paints and compositions; and the advantages accruing from the use of iron made learning to live with these problems a very worthwhile exercise. The iron ship was lighter and faster than its wooden counterpart; it provided more accommodation, easier stowage of cargo and safer transit for it. It stood up better to collision and stranding and was easier to make good after such an event; and with the invention of transverse bulkheads and double bottoms, the iron ship became altogether much safer than the wooden one had ever been. Finally it was cheaper – £13. 10*s*. a ton as against £16. 10*s*. for wood in the 1830s – and it was likely to become more so as iron became more plentiful and supplies of suitable timber dwindled.

PS *Aaron Manby*, 1822

The fouling problem did not arise in fresh water and, not surprisingly, iron boats and barges were used extensively on canals and inland waterways long before they appeared on salt water. John Wilkinson, a Shropshire ironmaster, is credited with the first craft built of wrought iron. She was a canal barge, 70 feet long, built in 1787 and used to carry coal, which she could shift at the then considerable rate of 32 tons a trip. The stem and stern posts in her were wood, but otherwise she was constructed of wrought iron plates, $\frac{5}{16}$ inch thick. Others followed at intervals without much significant development until 1818, when the *Vulcan*, a passenger boat built of sheets of iron riveted on to frames of flat iron bars, appeared on the Forth and Clyde Canal. The first iron-hulled steam vessel came four years later. She was the *Aaron Manby*, built at the Horsley Ironworks at Tipton in Staffordshire and sent in sections by canal to Rotherhithe. There she was reassembled and fitted with an oscillating engine driving a pair of feathering paddle-wheels, then navigated across the Channel to the River Seine, where she established a passenger service.

Napier and other pioneers

The second iron steamboat was also built at the Horsley Ironworks, again in sections, but this time she was assembled in Liverpool. This one was the *Marquis of Wellesley*, of 1825. She was driven by a 10 h.p. engine and ran successfully for many years on the River Shannon. After her came the *Aglaia*, 49 tons. Built by David Napier for service on Loch Eck, she was something of a compromise, having an iron bottom with wooden topsides; but by the 1830s iron shipbuilding had got beyond such hedging. It had also moved beyond Staffordshire and was established on the Clyde, the Mersey and the Thames. Other names besides Napier, and equally famous, were connected with it, among them Grantham, Laird, Fairbairn, Thomas Wingate, Ditchburn, Mare and the Clydeside pair Tod and Macgregor of whom more later. Laird's first was the *Alburkak*, 70 tons, 14 h.p., built in 1831 for service on the River Niger. She was followed by the *John Randolph*, 250 tons, the *Lady Lansdowne*, a 130-footer shipped to Ireland in sections and reassembled there, and the *Garryowen*, 263 tons, 80 h.p. This last was fitted with bulkheads and demonstrated the strength of this kind of construction by surviving two strandings and starting a new career on the African coast over thirty years later. Then came the *Rainbow*, 580 tons, which he built for the General Steam Navigation Company.

Meanwhile, from Fairbairn at Manchester, came the *Lord Dundas* and the *Manchester* and on the Thames, Maudslay, Sons and Field secured an order for four iron paddle-steamers to be used on the Ganges. These, the *Lord W. Bentinck*, the *Thames*, the *Megna* and the *Jumna*, were all 120 feet long, of 275 tons, with engines of 30 nominal h.p., and they were taken down and shipped out to India in sections. But the real growing-point was on the Clyde where Tod and Macgregor of Glasgow, having set up as engine-builders, added iron shipbuilding

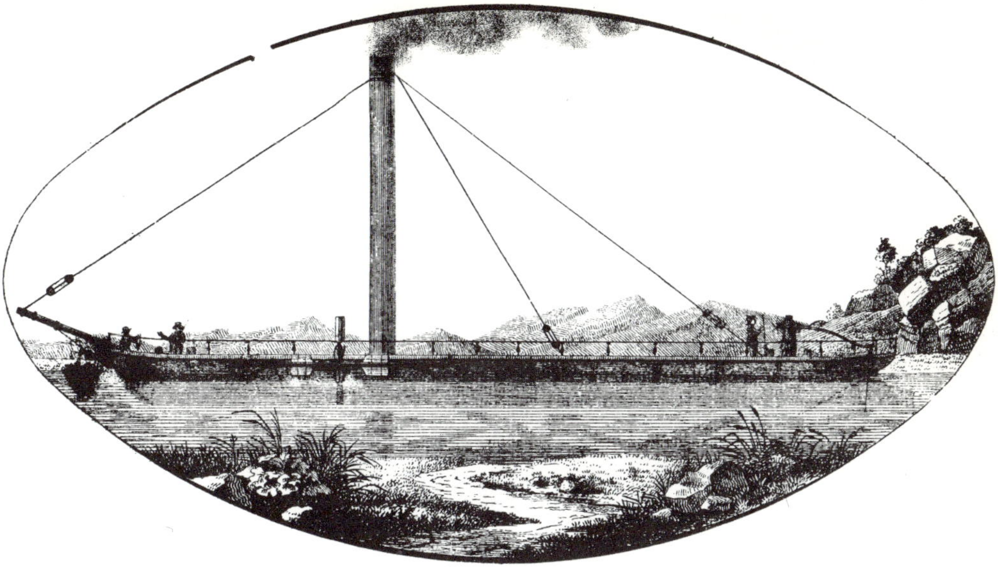

53 PS *Aaron Manby*, 1822. First iron-hulled steamship

to their interests. Beginning in 1835 with the *Vale of Leven*, 121 tons, they built bigger and bigger until in 1839 they produced the *Royal Sovereign*, 177 feet long, 446 tons and 220 h.p. and her sister ship the *Royal George*, for service between Liverpool and Glasgow. They were followed on the same route three years later by the even bigger *Princess Royal*, which was 194 feet long, and Smith reckons the success of these three 'went far to remove the prejudice against iron steamers'. It is his judgment that they, together with Laird's *Rainbow*, 'may be taken as the precursors of the ocean-going iron steamer'.

Nevertheless there was no runaway victory for iron as the basic material for shipbuilding. In 1850, out of all the new tonnage launched from British yards, only 10 per cent was of iron and even ten years after that, two out of every three tons was still being built of wood.

'Iron ship A1'

The first iron steamer registered at Lloyd's was the *Sirius*, 180 tons, built by Fairbairn at Millwall in 1837. In a sense this was only a tentative recognition and the seal of approval did not come till 1844, when the classification *Iron ship A1* was given to all vessels built under the inspection of the society's surveyors. A kind of grudging Government acceptance came two years later when an Act of Parliament was passed '. . . regulating the construction of sea-going steam vessels and for preventing the occurrence of accidents in steam navigation.' The most important of these regulations was one under which all iron steam vessels of 100 tons and over had to be divided into three watertight compartments by two transverse bulkheads, one just forward of the engine-room and the other immediately abaft it.

THE SCREW

Developed almost parallel with the ocean-going iron steamship, came the screw propeller, which has been described as 'the greatest of all innovations in the propulsion of ships by mechanical power'.

The screw, like the wheel, had been about for a long time; and successive generations of men had used it for various purposes since the name of Archimedes was tagged on to it in the third century BC. The earliest suggestion that it might be used to propel ships is recorded in a patent taken out by Joseph Bramah in 1785 (see p. 25). Nine years after that, William Littleton patented a screw with three blades and in 1800 Edward Shorter produced one that actually moved a ship, but it was manipulated by a man-powered capstan. The first truly successful experiment with screw propulsion came in 1804 when, as noted earlier, the American Colonel John Stevens drove his *Little Juliana*, a boat 24 feet long, round New York harbour with twin screws and reached the remarkable speed of 4 miles an hour. Among other inventors in the field before the 1830s were Trevithick, Millington, de Lisle, Perkins and Samuel Brown; but the credit for solving the practical problems involved in screw propulsion for ships belongs in varying degrees to John Ericsson (1803–89), Francis Pettit Smith (1808–74), James Lowe (1796–1866), Bennet Woodcroft (1803–79) and George Blaxland. They met with the same kind of official obstruction and educated scepticism as the advocates of iron ships had encountered and one writer of the period summed it up as follows:

> The whole engineering corps of the empire was arrayed in opposition to it, alleging that it was constructed on erroneous principles and full of practical defects. [Woodcroft, p. 94]

Prejudice and limited facilities apart, there were, of course, some very real problems which might be grouped under three headings; those concerned with the size and shape of the propeller, those connected with the driving of it, and those its adoption created for the ship designer. These last included the question of *thrust*, the provision of an adequate stern gland, and finally, the problem of minimizing the effects of vibration.

It was Smith and Ericsson, working independently of each other, who produced the world's first practical screw-propelled ships and Smith's patent taken out on 31 May 1836 was just six weeks ahead of Ericsson's. The specification was for a device which was to

> . . . consist of a sort of screw or worm made to revolve rapidly under water, in a recess or open space formed in that part of the after-part of the vessel, commonly called the dead-rising or dead wood of the run . . . it might be arranged singly in an open space . . . or induplicate with one on each side of the deadwood, or otherwise placed more forward or more aft, or more or less deep in the water. . . .

SS *Francis Smith*, 1836

That same year Smith had the *Francis Smith*, a steamboat of 6 tons built at Wapping and fitted it with a wooden screw. After trials in which part of the propeller was broken off, he changed to a metal one and in 1837 drove her from London to Ramsgate and Folkestone, a remarkable achievement for a vessel powered by a steam engine with a cylinder only 6 inches in diameter and a stroke of 15 inches.

With this kind of achievement to talk about, he was able to obtain financial backing and a syndicate was formed under the name of The Ship Propeller Company to acquire the patents and exploit the invention. The first step was to build a commercially viable craft in which to demonstrate the advantages of the screw propeller over the paddle-wheel, and a ship of 240 tons was laid down for the purpose. The original intention was to call her the 'Propeller', but she was ultimately named *Archimedes* after the Greek geometer. She was 106 feet long between perpendiculars, 22½ feet beam and drew between 9 and 10 feet of water. Her power-unit was an engine with two

54 SS *Archimedes*, 240 tons, 80 nominal h.p. off the Nore light vessel May 1839

cylinders 37 inches in diameter with a 3-foot stroke. It drove the propeller shaft through gearing at 140 revolutions per minute to 26 revolutions of the engine and was rated at 80 h.p. The boiler pressure was 6 lb. per square inch. The engines were built by Rennie, the ship itself by Henry Wimhurst.

The *Archimedes* began to show her paces in the spring of 1839, steaming from the Thames to Bristol with calls at the principal south coast ports. At Dover she was put up against HMS *Widgeon*, a paddler and the fastest in that particular section of the Royal Navy. The trial was official and the report of it, made to the Board of Admiralty by Captain E. Chapell and Thomas Lloyd, grudgingly admitted that the power of the screw was equal, 'if not superior to that of the ordinary paddle-wheel', and that contrary to the current myth, it made steering easier; but it drew attention to the rapid wear of the gear-wheels and the excessive amount of noise they made. Smith promptly proposed to meet this criticism by using spiral gearing.

Following a run round the main home ports, the *Archimedes* made a voyage to Oporto; but after this success, she ran out of luck, blew up her boiler, broke a crankshaft and ran ashore on Beachy Head all in the same twelve months. That was in 1840 and seven years later the engines were taken out of her and she became a sailing ship. She is said to have cost £10,000 to build and Woodcroft estimates the company lost some £50,000 on the project; but Pettit Smith's story, unlike that of his ship and most other pioneers, had a happy ending,

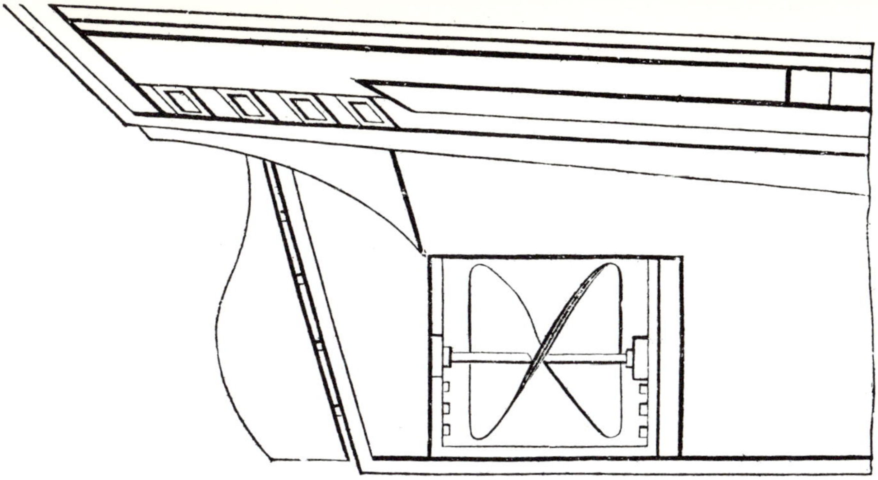

55 Screw propeller from the *Archimedes*

for his devotion to screw propulsion earned him the nickname of 'Screw Smith' and a knighthood as well as a place in history.

SS *Francis B. Ogden*, 1836

The other patentee, John Ericsson, was born in Sweden and held a commission in the Swedish Army. His real interest, however, was in mechanics and coming to London he obtained a partnership in a well-known engineering firm which became Braithwaites and Ericsson. His ideas received even rougher treatment at the hands of the Admiralty than Pettit Smith's had done. Building a boat 45 feet long by 8 feet beam, he equipped it with two propellers each 5 feet 3 inches in diameter. Smith describes the arrangement as follows:

> . . . [it] consisted of a short drum, like a belt pulley with blades around its circumference. He used two propellers, a right-handed and a left-handed one, the outer being fixed to the propeller shaft, revolving in a sleeve which carried the inner propeller. The sleeve was driven by toothed gearing and the propellers revolved in opposite directions as they do in a modern torpedo.

Ericsson named this craft the *Francis B. Ogden* after a friend, for many years United States consul at Liverpool, and invited the Lords of the Admiralty to take an excursion in her. Their Lordships were reluctant to trust themselves aboard the little steamer, but agreed to their barge being lashed alongside and towed by her.

An august party which included Sir Charles Adam, senior Lord at the Admiralty, Sir William Symonds, Surveyor of the Royal Navy, Captain Beaufort the hydrographer and other scientific moguls duly boarded the gilded barge at Somerset House and the *Francis B. Ogden* set off, towing her alongside. The excursion went as far as Limehouse and back and Ericsson's brain-child attained a speed of 10 miles an hour, barge and all; but all the inventor got out of it was a polite letter a few days later in which Captain Beaufort regretted having to inform him 'that their Lordships had been certainly very much disappointed' at the result of the experiment. No reason was given in the letter for this extraordinary decision, but at a subsequent dinner-party Sir William Symonds was less reticent and explained

> . . . that even if the propeller had the power of propelling a vessel, it would be found altogether useless in practice, because the power being applied in the stern, it would be absolutely impossible to make the vessel steer.
> [quoted Woodcroft, p. 93]

SS *Robert F. Stockton*, 1839

At that, Ericsson gave up the Lords of the Admiralty as hopelessly committed to their wooden hulls and paddle-wheels and turned to America for backing and encouragement, finding all he needed in the person of Captain Robert F. Stockton of the United States Navy who, says Woodcroft, 'is entitled to the credit of being the first naval officer who heard, understood and dared to act upon the suggestions of Ericsson as to the application of the propeller to ships of war'. He had a new iron ship built by Lairds of Birkenhead. Named the *Robert F. Stockton*, she was 70 feet long and 10 feet in the beam with a draught of 6 feet 9 inches; she had engines with cylinders 16 inches in diameter and an 18-inch stroke, and the Ericsson screw propeller 76 inches in diameter is reputed to have driven her through the water on the Thames below Blackwall at between 11 and 12 miles an hour. The *Robert F. Stockton* was sailed across to the United States in 1839 taking forty days for the passage, and the following year with her name changed to *New Jersey* she was sold for service as a tugboat on the Delaware River in which capacity she was a great success, particularly in the winter ice.

John Ericsson subsequently became an honoured American citizen and Woodcroft sums him up as follows:

> . . . Captain Ericsson accomplished for the screw propeller in America and in England, what Fulton did for the paddle-wheel in the former, and Bell in the latter country, namely its practical introduction.
>
> [p. 102]

HMS *Rattler* v. HMS *Alecto*

Meanwhile Wimhurst, who had built the *Archimedes* for Screw Smith's Ship Propeller Company, came up with a bigger steamer which was named the *Novelty* and sent on a voyage from Liverpool to Constantinople with 420 tons of cargo aboard. She thus became 'the parent of the screw-driven cargo boat'. Then with Ericsson building the screw-propelled *Princeton* for the United States Navy and Normand the *Napoleon* for the French, the Lords of the Admiralty at last stirred themselves in the matter. They had building at Sheerness a sloop called the *Ardent*, which had been laid down as a paddle-steamer but was altered for screw propulsion before her launch and renamed the *Rattler*. Launched in the spring of 1843, she had a displacement of 1,078 tons and was fitted with a Maudslay 'Siamese' engine of 437 indicated h.p. which drove the propeller shaft through gears. It was this ship which finally proved beyond all doubt and peradventure the superiority of the screw over the paddle. After exhaustive but largely inconclusive trials against the paddle-sloop *Alecto*, 800 tons and 200 nominal h.p., the two ships were lashed together stern to stern. Then the *Rattler* with her engines stopped, was towed backwards by the paddler. When she had got going flat out, the *Rattler* went ahead on her engines and not only pulled the other ship up dead but finished towing her astern at 2½ miles an hour with her paddles still churning for all she was worth.

I. K. Brunel, 1806–59

One of the first marine engineers and ship designers to be convinced of both the efficacy of the screw and the advantages to be gained by building of iron, was I. K. Brunel, the man who built the *Great Western* and conquered the Atlantic Ocean with her for steam navigation. Of Isambard Kingdom Brunel, as of all near-legendary heroes, endless stories are told; stories of his eccentricity, his courage, his ruthlessness and his humanity and many of them must be apocryphal; but there is one thing about him that no one has ever

56 Isambard Kingdom Brunel, 1806–59. Shipbuilder extraordinary

57 [*opposite*] SS *Great Britain* off Lundy island on her maiden voyage

questioned – his genius. Uninhibited by traditionalism, his thinking on any subject to which he turned his mind was breath-taking in its sweep and freedom; but what was more important perhaps, he had the personal magnetism, the charm that enabled him to convince other people his ideas were sound and worth backing to the limit. Consequently, his achievement, from entering his father's engineering business at the age of seventeen till his death thirty-six years later, was enormous and made him known all over the world as 'the Little Giant'. Among other things, he drove the first tunnel under the Thames, and served as engineer to the Great Western Railway in which capacity he supervised the design and construction of all the tunnels and bridges on the London to Bristol route. He built the bridges over the Thames at Maidenhead, over the Wye at Chepstow and over the Tamar at Saltash in Devon; was responsible for improving the docks at Bristol, Cardiff and North Sunderland; put up the idea of compartmented freight cars; pioneered railway telegraphy; proposed that a canal should be cut through the Isthmus of Panama; designed and built the old Hungerford Suspension Bridge; designed and started to build the Clifton Suspension Bridge, but died before it was completed. For him, it seemed, nothing was *impossible*; either that or the word had no place in his vocabulary; and his attitude to all

problems and difficulties is very well summed up in his comment on the screw propeller:

> We must adopt *as a principle not to be departed from* that all mechanical difficulties of construction must give way, must in fact be lost sight of, in determining the most perfect form – if we find that the screw determined upon *cannot* be made (but what cannot be made?), then it is quite time enough to try another form; though even then *my rule* would be to try again at making it. [quoted V. Wegg-Prosser, p. 6]

SS *Great Britain*, 1843

Bridge-builder, railway engineer, tunnel-driver, canal-cutter, constructor of docks, inventor, organizer extraordinary – Brunel was all these things and many more; but the concern here is with Brunel the shipbuilder and forward-thinker, the man who saw five, ten, in one case almost fifty years ahead of his time and translated his visions into viable realities. One of them was the *Great Britain*, the first iron steamer to be employed on the Atlantic.

Built like the *Great Western*, by Patterson of Bristol in 1838 and originally conceived as a wooden paddler, Brunel took his time about her and after working on the design for fifteen months, decided to build her of iron. On 19 July 1839 the keel was laid in a dry dock constructed especially for her. Since she was to be almost four times the size of anything built up till then, she was tentatively named the *Mammoth*, the more familiar name being given to her before she was completed. More important than the change of name was the decision taken in November 1840 to cancel the order for her paddle-engines and fit her instead with a screw propeller and the appropriate machinery for driving it.

The dimensions of Brunel's marvel were:

Length of keel	289 feet
Length overall	320 feet
Beam	51 feet
Depth from upper deck to keel	31 feet 4 inches
Loaded draught	16 feet
Tonnage (old measurement)	3,500

She had accommodation for 360 passengers and a dining-saloon big enough to seat 20 more than that. Her crew numbered 130 hands all told and she had stowage for 1,100 tons of bunker coal. Her propelling machinery was as remarkable as the rest of her, and a model of it can be seen in the Science Museum at South Kensington. Smith describes it as consisting of:

> . . . four direct-acting cylinders, each 88 inches diameter and of 6 ft stroke, placed at an angle of 33° with the vertical, driving an overhanging crankshaft which carried a drum 18¼ ft diameter and 38 inches wide, which by means of four flat pitch chains, drove a smaller drum about 6 ft diameter, fixed on the propeller shaft. . . .

She had flue boilers with twenty-four furnaces and a fire-bar area of 288 feet superficial. The boilers were worked at 5 lb. per square inch and at 18 revolutions a minute, the engine developed about 2,000 h.p. which gave the ship a service speed of 12 knots.

Up till that time no ship had ever had such enormous strength built into her. Her keel was made of flat iron plates, $\frac{7}{8}$ inch thick and 20 inches wide, welded into lengths of 50 feet. The frames in her were set as little as 18 inches and never more than 24 inches apart and the shell-plating was nowhere less than $\frac{3}{8}$ inch thick and often as much as $\frac{11}{16}$ inch. She was divided into compartments by five transverse bulkheads and further strengthened by eleven longitudinal girders under an inner bottom.

Instead of being punched out at speed by machine as is done today, every rivet-hole in all this massive structure had to be drilled separately by hand and each rivet knocked up in the same way; and the building of her threw up many other problems, demanding the development of so many new techniques and the invention of so many special tools, that it took a long time to accomplish and it was not until 19 July 1843 that she was floated out of her dock. The event, performed by the Prince Consort himself no less, was preceded by an intensive publicity campaign with *The Illustrated London News* leading the chorus. The ship, declared that famous nineteenth-century glossy,

> . . . is of unparalleled vastness, her actual tonnage being some hundreds of tons more than that of any ship ever built, which circumstance, conjoined with her peculiarities of material and construction, must render her completion an important event in the records of engineering and mechanical skill. [15 July 1843]

Kirkcaldy, looking back on her from the turn of the century, is more sober in his judgment though no less enthusiastic. For him, the *Great Britain* was not so much *built* as *created* and he is lyrical about her success, her strength and her fine qualities as a sea boat. According to him, she cost upwards of £120,000 to build, but even though she brought little profit to her original owners and leaving aside her profound influence on every aspect of marine engineering and ship design, her long and useful career proved her to be worth every penny put into her and very much more.

After extensive trials closely linked with the publicity campaign, she sailed from Liverpool on 26 July 1845 on her maiden voyage to New York. Aboard her were over 300 passengers, who were charged £30, £25 or £20 each according to the class of their one-way ticket. In spite of strong westerly gales and fog, she made the passage in fourteen days twenty-one hours and received a tumultuous welcome. The rest of her career is summarized below:

Voyages 1 to 4 6 13 and 15	Liverpool to New York
5	Not completed; ran aground in Dundrum Bay, Ireland, subsequently refloated and towed back to Birkenhead

7 to 9 11 14 16 to 44	Liverpool to Melbourne, via Cape of Good Hope
10 and 12	Trooping in the Crimea and Indian Mutiny
45 and 46 (under sail with her engines removed)	Liverpool to San Francisco, via the Horn
47	Left Penarth for San Francisco 6 February 1886 and after a whole month trying to beat round the Horn was towed back to the Falkland Islands, ran aground and was declared a total loss. She ultimately became a store hulk and then a coal hulk
48	In 1970: towed back to Bristol on a pontoon

The record is unique and as a ship the *Great Britain* was indeed a total success; but, too long in the building, too expensive to maintain and run – she burned between 35 and 50 tons of coal a day – to some extent she cost the Great Western Steamship Company their chance of beating Cunard for the Atlantic mail subsidy and was one of the factors that forced the firm into liquidation in 1852.

Problems outstanding

Meanwhile throughout the 1840s, Woodcroft, Pettit Smith, Penn and others were working at the three great problems immediately facing marine engineers, (*a*) propeller design; (*b*) thrust; and (*c*) the stern gland.

The controversy that raged round propellers was particularly fierce and Bennet Woodcroft was at the heart of it as the following extract from *The Times* of 5 July 1848 shows:

> Woolwich, July 5: The *Minx* steam-vessel, one hundred horse-power, went down the river last week, with thirteen different modifications of screw propellers, for which she is fitted, one shipped, and the others to be tested, to ascertain their relative qualities in giving speed to the vessel . . . the whole thirteen were tried with the greatest care, as many as thirty passages being made in one day up and down the measured mile at Long Reach, commencing the trials at four o'clock in the morning and continuing them until dusk on Thursday, Friday and Saturday last. . . .

The trials were a triumph for Woodcroft's *increasing-pitch screw*

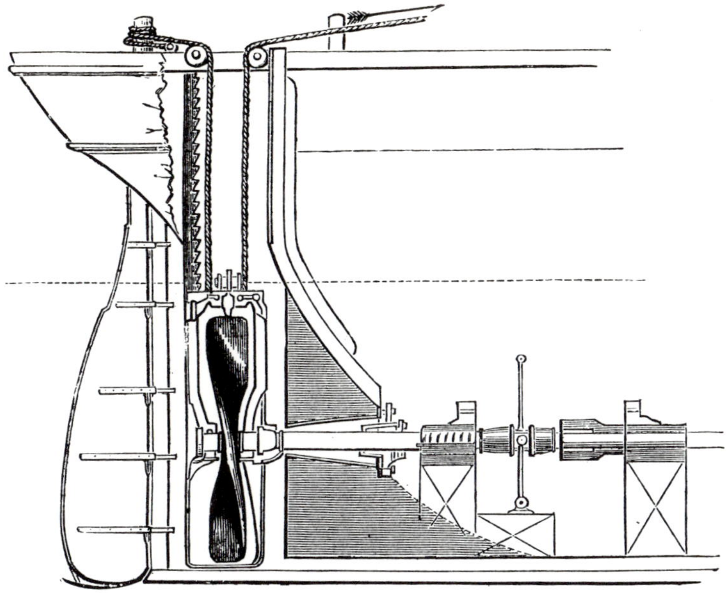

58 Drawing of ship's stern showing stern gland and thrust block

with which the *Minx* registered a good 9 knots for the expenditure of less power and fewer revolutions of the engine than with the conventional *uniform-pitch screw*. Nevertheless, the arguments and the experiments continued and they still go on today, for the ultimate propeller, perfect in size, shape and pitch for every ship in all conditions and circumstances, has yet to come.

The problem of thrust was more amenable. In the beginning while engine power was still relatively small, it was tackled in a number of ways. Where the propeller shaft was driven through gears, as in the *Rattler* for example, the thrust was taken by a plate 'opposed to the end of the shaft'. This was also the arrangement in the *Great Britain*; her shaft pressing against an iron plate 2 feet in diameter cooled with a constant stream of water. With direct-acting engines, however, there was a vertical *pushing post* built into the ship between keel and deck, or the thrust might be taken on the stern post itself. None of these arrangements were entirely satisfactory and with the power of engines steadily increasing, other methods were tried until eventually the multi-collar thrust block was evolved and universally adopted.

But of all the problems thrown up by the introduction of screw propulsion, the toughest was undoubtedly that of the stern gland, which is the circular opening built into the ship's stern frame to take the shaft from the propeller through into the thrust block and the engines. In the early days, a long brass bush or sleeve was used for the stern bearing, but brass was too soft and wore away at an alarming rate; the sloop *Malacca*, for instance, lost metal at the rate of 5 lb. a day. In the end it was Penn, working in collaboration with Pettit Smith, who found the answer. Organizing a test shaft running in a tank of water, he tried out bearings made from a wide range of metal alloys and wood, including lignum vitae, the hardest and heaviest of all timbers and one with the unique property of self-lubrication. After exhaustive tests, he found that iron working on lignum vitae was the perfect answer. With it, the under-water bearing would carry pressures of up to 8,000 lb. per square inch. The invention was immediately successful and the record indicates that within two years of its introduction more than 200 ships had changed their brass stern tubes for lignum-vitae bearings.

SS *City of Glasgow*

Though Brunel's *Great Britain* had demonstrated the strength of the iron hull and the practicality of the screw propeller, she was a maverick, a rogue, outside the main stream of development in steam navigation, and her like was never built again. It was another and less sensational ship that became the prototype of the modern ocean liner. She came in response to the greatest pressure to which sea-borne transport had ever been subjected. The late 1840s and early 1850s were stirring times in every sense of the word. In 1846 England repealed her Corn Laws which had imposed tariffs on imports of foreign wheat to protect the Irish smallholder and tenant-farmer, who 'grew wheat to pay the rent and potatoes to feed himself and his family'. That same year the potato crop failed and there was famine in the land. Large-scale evictions followed, hundreds of thousands died of starvation, and those who survived and had the means, got out. The number of people going overseas to try and make a new and better life for themselves was already running at about 70,000 a year in 1840 and then with the Irish exodus it swelled to a great wave that threatened to swamp existing transport systems and facilities. In 1849 the discovery of gold in California added its quota to the flood, and similar strikes in Australia two years later turned it into a veritable torrent which trebled the population of that far-off land in three short years.

Very few of these potential passengers could afford the current steamship fares, which even on the relatively short North Atlantic routes were running at twenty to thirty guineas a head, and for the majority of them the only hope was a steerage passage in a sailing ship for which the going rate was four to six guineas. This was a daunting prospect. Some of the packets carried as many as 700 steerage passengers and the duration of the ordeal was entirely unpredictable. For instance, the *Diamond* was 100 days going from Liverpool to New York one winter and 17 out of her 180 steerage passengers died of starvation on the trip.

It was against this background that the Clydeside firm of Tod and Macgregor built their famous *City of Glasgow* (1,600 tons) in 1850. She was neither big by Brunel's standards nor fast by Cunard's, but her advent marked the beginning of an epoch in ocean travel. Built of iron, she was 237 feet long by 34 feet beam and was equipped with 'two lever beam-engines of 350 horsepower' driving a 13-foot propeller with an 18-foot pitch through steeple gears with a steam pressure of 10 lb. per square inch. She logged $8\frac{1}{2}$ knots on her trials.

In a way, the *City of Glasgow* was a statement of faith. She came at a time when the first essential in steamer design was great speed, the second elaborate accommodation and facilities to lure passengers from the sailing packets and competing steamship lines. Running costs came into the picture a long way down the list and economic viability nowhere. Consequently the wooden paddlers were expensive to run and maintain; much of their carrying capacity was taken up by the huge engines and boilers and space for bunkers to supply them. Because of this, there was little room left in them for freight-paying cargo and it was generally accepted that no regular steamship service could be kept going without high fares and a Government mail subsidy. Tod and Macgregor believed this was a fallacy and built the *City of Glasgow* to prove it so.

59 Below deck in an emigrant ship

In her, economic viability was the prime consideration and her design was based on careful costing with a view to striking a balance between the requirements of the trade and the return it offered. Consequently a more rational approach was adopted to questions of speed, size and passenger facilities and the result was an entirely new type of ship, which in the end revolutionized ocean travel. The following comparison between her and the Cunard Company's contemporary wooden paddler, *Asia*, indicates why:

	Asia	*City of Glasgow*
Tonnage	2,250	1,600
Coal consumption, tons per day	76	20
Cargo capacity, tons	500	1,200
Passengers, accommodation for:		
Cabin classes	160	137
Steerage	None	400

The reduction in the fuel bill, after allowing for the longer passage due to lower average speed, amounted to about 60 per cent. This was

60 Emigrants embarking at Portsmouth

an enormously significant saving which was demonstrated by a couple of Glasgow–New York voyages under the builders' ownership; and when the extra earning capacity in both passengers and freight was added to it, there was no doubt about Tod and Macgregor having proved their point.

The Inman Line

The first man to act on it was William Inman who was a partner in a firm managing sailing packets out of Liverpool. He bought the *City of Glasgow* and founded the Liverpool and Philadelphia Steam Ship Company, famous on the North Atlantic for forty-odd years as the Inman Line.

The new company's first important decision was to cut the existing transatlantic fares to twenty-two guineas for first class and thirteen guineas for second class; its next, to order a sister to their fine new ship. She came in 1851 – the *City of Manchester*, 1,900 tons – and the following year they began carrying emigrants as steerage passengers at eight guineas a head. They were the first steamship line to do so and the record insists that they offered 'much improved conditions'. Steerage passengers were required to furnish their own bed and bedding, mess-tins, cutlery and water-can, but a company poster circulated in New York in 1863 undertook to provide each of them with 'a separate berth to sleep in' and promised that the women would 'be placed in rooms by themselves'. The company was legally bound to feed its steerage passengers according to a minimum scale, but apparently ignored this and offered them 'as much provisions and water as they may wish to use,' the published *Bill of Fare* being as follows:

> *Breakfast at Eight o'clock*: Coffee, sugar and fresh bread and butter, or biscuit and butter or oatmeal porridge and molasses.
>
> *Dinner at One o'clock*: Beef or pork and soup, with potatoes and bread, or fish and potatoes, according to the day of the week, and plum-pudding on Sunday.
>
> *Supper at Six o'clock*: Tea and sugar, biscuit and butter.
>
> [quoted Gibbs, app. D, pp. 364–5]

So everybody knew what to expect in the way of food, but the 'separate berth' was a rather flattering description of the accommodation, which 'consisted of tiers of wooden shelves in airless compartments below the waterline'. Here the hapless passengers slept side by side anything from six to twelve deep; but the sexes were duly segregated, each place numbered and allocated, so strictly speaking there was no deception about the advertisement. Nevertheless, one is irresistibly reminded of the slave-ships except that here there was just a little more space per head and no manacles; but the steerage passengers, like the slaves, were only allowed on deck at specified times and even then confined to extremely limited areas of it.

These *much improved* conditions were general throughout the trade; but we know the plight of the steerage passenger aboard a sailing ship was infinitely worse, and the fact that through all those years both steamers and clippers continued to sail with holds more or less crammed with people, shows how desperate they were to get out and make a fresh start.

Although Inman had got his sums right and read the signs and portents with a remarkable degree of acumen, he could do no more than the next man about the imponderables and in 1854 his luck ran out. In March of that year, the *City of Glasgow* sailed from Liverpool with a total of 480 souls, passengers and crew, aboard. She was neither seen nor heard of again. Then five months later, his *City of Philadelphia*, 2,200 tons, on her maiden voyage from Liverpool was wrecked near Cape Race, ten days out and became a total loss, though all her people were saved.

The Inman Line, however, was so soundly based and so shrewdly managed that it not only survived these disasters but lived down the adverse publicity they engendered and went on to become a serious challenge to even the best of the North Atlantic steamship operators. In 1856–7, i.e. little more than two years later, out of the 200,000 people who went to America from England, the Inman Line carried a total of 70,000, which is near enough one in every three; but what is perhaps more important, they set new standards in fares, in ship design, in passenger facilities and in management techniques to which even the lordly Cunard Company in some degree had eventually to conform.

The emigrant trade

But others were getting in on what now looked more like a lucrative investment than the crazy gamble steam navigation had hitherto been and many famous house-flags first appeared in iron screw steamers on the North Atlantic during this decade. Among them were:

The Allan Line, floated in Montreal in 1853 as the Montreal Ocean SS Company, to run a regular service between Liverpool and Quebec/Montreal, and in 1856 granted a Government mail subsidy of £25,000 per annum. Their first ship was the iron screw steamer *Canadian*, 1,750 tons.

The Hamburg Amerikanische Paketfahrt Aktien Gesellschaft, known as 'Hapag' for short. This German company was already running a fleet of sailing ships between Hamburg and New York, each of them carrying 20 saloon passengers and 200 steerage. They were averaging forty days out and twenty-nine home. In 1854, inspired no doubt by the success of the *City of Glasgow*, they ordered two iron screw steamers from Caird of Greenock. They were the *Borussia* and the *Hammonia*, sister ships of 2,000 tons.

The Norddeutscher Lloyd, more familiarly known as the North German Lloyd or simply by the initials, NDL, was started in 1857 with three iron screw steamers – *Adler*, *Mowe* and *Falke* – and a year later inaugurated their Bremerhaven–New York service with the first *Bremen*.

Compagnie Générale Transatlantique, famous now as the CGT, began operations in 1862 with the iron screw steamer *Floride*, 1,800 tons and her sister ship, the *Louisiana*. But somebody with a lot of influence had doubts and in the same year, the new company ordered eight iron paddle-steamers from Scotts of Greenock. The first of them was the *Washington*, 3,200 tons, driven by standard two-cylinder side-lever engines. The CGT persisted for some time with paddlers and their *Napoleon III*, 3,400 tons, completed by the Thames Ironworks in 1866 was the last paddle-driven steamer designed and built for the North Atlantic trade. It is interesting to note that the tonnage of the paddlers was twice that of the contemporary screw steamers.

The National Line, founded in 1863, made a completely new and extremely significant approach to the business of ocean transport by steamship. At this time, generally speaking, trade westward across the North Atlantic consisted of compact, high-cost, manufactured goods that were worth the high freight charges for the sake of quicker transit and firm delivery dates; what went eastward was in the main cheap, bulky raw materials, for which low transit charges were much more important than speedy delivery. This state of affairs suited the wooden paddlers with their limited cargo capacity admirably. They concentrated on passengers and mails, took the cream of the cargo offering, charged the maximum freight-rate it would stand and left the rest to the sailing ships. National built their ships bigger and slower, made them cheaper to run and went for the bulk cargoes in a big way. They installed accommodation for a limited number of saloon passengers almost as an afterthought, and compensated for the lack of bulk cargoes westward by filling the empty holds with emigrants stowed in temporary sleeping-berths. Eastward they carried anything they could get, including live cattle.

The Liverpool and Great Western SS Company, widely known in its day as the Guion Line, came into being in 1866 and followed a similar course. It was founded by the American owners of the Black Star Line of sailing ships to meet the overwhelming competition of the iron screw steamers in the emigrant trade, acting presumably on the time-honoured principle of 'if you can't beat them, join them'.

61 SS *Sabrina* inaugurating a new graving dock at Jarrow, 1865

Guion's first ship was the *Manhattan* and she sailed from Liverpool for New York on 7 August 1866, flying the Black Star house-flag and the red ensign. The following year, Guion and National between them landed 61,000 emigrants in New York.

The main reason for the development of the iron screw steamship being concentrated on the eastern side of the Atlantic in this period, was that American builders still had to rely on imported iron. This made the cost of iron hulls prohibitive and even screw-propelled American ships continued to be built of timber which was cheap and plentiful. But the screw propeller in the wooden hull was never successful and for a while American shipbuilding genius concerned itself with the sailing ship, then reaching towards its ultimate. Gibbs records that 'from 1867 until 1895 only five new steamers entered the trans-atlantic trade under the Stars and Stripes'.

The combined effect of the iron hull, the screw propeller and the mass emigration of the 1850s was as powerful and far-reaching on other routes as on the North Atlantic and nowhere more so than on the direct run to Australia.

General Screw Steam Shipping Company

The first leg of this route, to the Cape of Good Hope was difficult enough because of bunkering and other supply problems, but a firm called the General Screw Steam Shipping Company undertook it with the help of a Government mail contract. They had three iron screw ships built by Mare of Blackwall and engined by Maudslays and named them the *Bosphorus*, the *Hellespont* and the *Propontis*. The first of them, the *Bosphorus*, sailed from Plymouth on 16 December 1850 for Cape Town. The ships – 175 feet long and 560 tons – were small and either for that reason or some other now lost in the mists, the venture failed, the ships first being taken up by the Government as transports and subsequently converted into sailing ships.

Cunard's SS *Australian*

Two years later Cunard took a hand with the iron screw ship *Australian*, built by Denny at Dumbarton. She was 236 feet long, 34 feet beam and equipped with geared beam engines of 576 indicated h.p., but in spite of her greater size and more powerful engines, she took 221 days for the round voyage and that attempt to establish a regular service was abandoned.

European and Australian Royal Mail Steam Navigation Company

The demand however was insistent and the next man to respond to it was the big-thinking, creative-building Isambard Kingdom Brunel. In 1852, acting for the European and Australian Royal Mail Steam Navigation Company, he designed two screw steamers. Built by Scott Russell, they were the *Victoria* and the *Adelaide*, 261 feet long, 38 feet beam and 1,350 tons gross. They had detachable screw propellers which gave them a speed under steam of 11·6 knots on a consumption of 37 tons of coal a day and left them free to take full advantage of the trade winds. The *Victoria*, first away, went from Gravesend to Adelaide in sixty days including two days lost coaling at St Vincent – a performance which can only be fully appreciated when seen against the sailing-ship norms of her day, set out in the following table:

Year	*Longest passage (days)*	*Shortest passage (days)*	*Average (days)*
1847	159	99	121
1848	159	94	119

Altogether in the ten years from 1840 to 1850 a total of 520 sailing ships made the England–Australia passage and all but a few took 121 to 130 days in which to do it.

SS *Great Eastern*, 18,914 tons

But it wasn't enough merely to half the passage time of the sailing ships; the steamers that did it had also to be economically viable and Brunel's latest creations came nowhere near to meeting this requirement. They were, in fact, so expensive to run that no amount of managing genius could make them pay in the Australian trade. Pondering this indisputable fact, Brunel came up with the *Great Eastern*, the most remarkable ship ever built and one of the greatest achievements ever made in marine engineering. Quite simply, he concluded the first Australian venture had failed because the ships were too small and had to stop at too many extremely expensive coaling stations on the way. He proposed to build a ship six times the size of anything else afloat – say about 20,000 tons – which, once under way, would be more easily propelled than steamers of the usual size and thus attain a greater average speed with a smaller consumption of coal. Fifteen knots was the speed he envisaged and that would cut the passage time to a mere forty-five days. Moreover, she would be big enough to carry bunkers to take her all the way to Australia and shift so much cargo and passengers per voyage that he confidently predicted she would pay dividends of about 40 per cent.

It sounded like a pipe-dream, but he raised the money and his ship, which he then called the *Leviathan* began building at Millwall

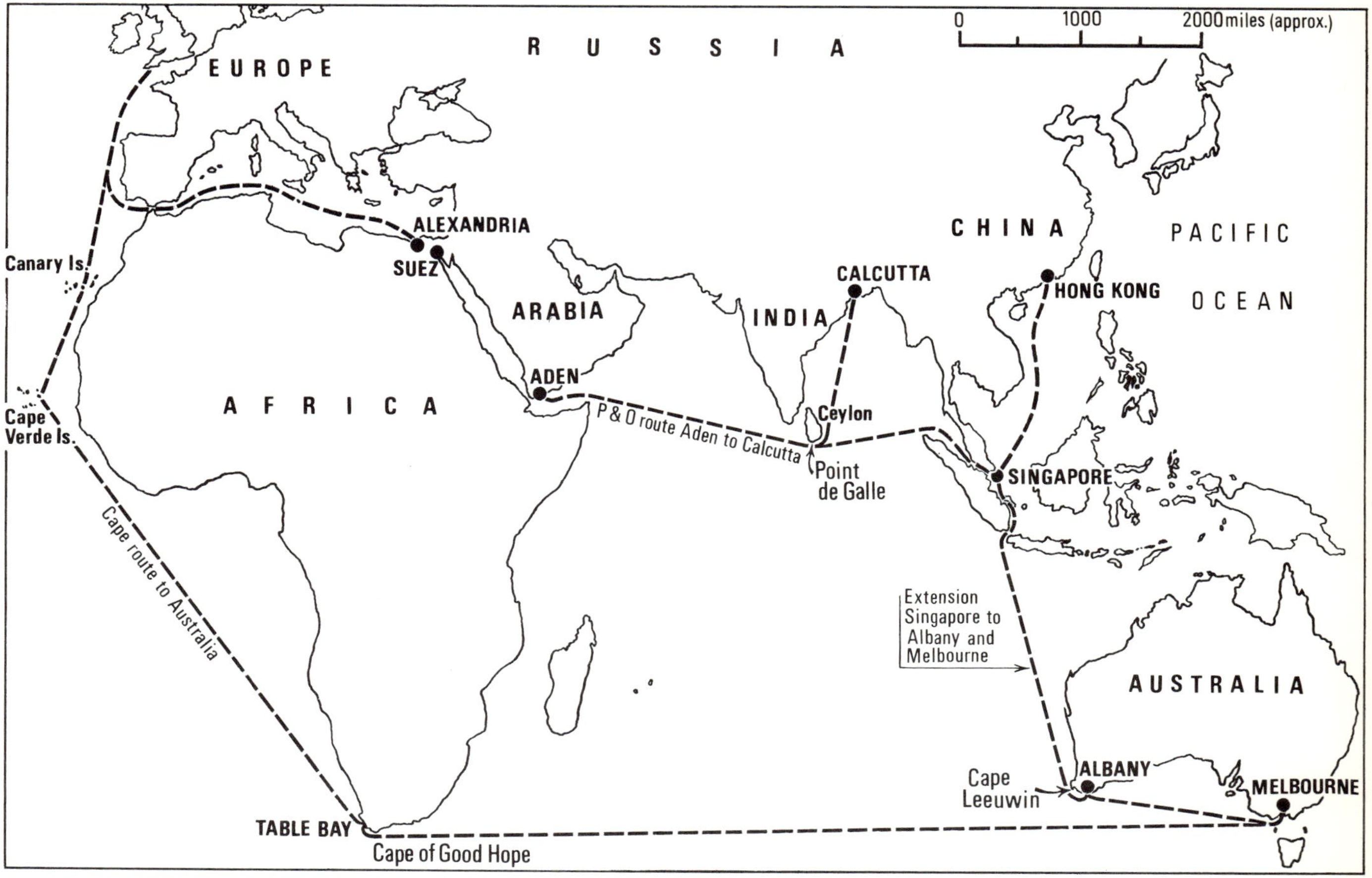

MAP No. 7 The Cape route to Australia with P & O extensions.

on 1 May 1854. The biggest ship ever built at that time was 3,300 tons gross and 375 feet long. Brunel's masterpiece came off the drawing-board with the following vital statistics:

Length	692 feet
Beam	82·5 feet
Tonnage	18,914 gross tons
Bunker capacity	10,000 tons
Cargo capacity	6,000 tons
Accommodation	4,000 passengers
Capacity as a transport	10,000 troops
Displacement	27,384 tons
Power of screw engines	4,886 i.h.p.
Power of paddle engines	3,411 i.h.p.
Speed	14·5 knots

It will be noted that she was equipped with both paddle-wheels and a screw propeller, a truly remarkable feature, but no more so than the immense strength built into her. Up till then the methods used in constructing iron steamers were still largely adaptations of wooden shipbuilding techniques; but for Brunel, iron demanded its own ideas and he borrowed them from the bridge-builders, Robert Stephenson and Fairbairn. Structurally she was cellular, with a double shell from water-line to keel and no less than 30 inches between the inner and outer plating. The main deck was also cellular and besides several longitudinal bulkheads, there was a transverse one for every 60 feet of her length, those at the bow and stern being double.

She was built parallel to the river and it has been estimated that her total weight lying there was not less than 12,000 tons. This immense load was borne on two cradles, each 80 feet square resting on slipways 200 feet long with a drop of 1 in 14. The first attempt to launch her failed and fourteen months later after many abortive efforts, she floated off herself on an abnormally high tide. That was on the 31 January 1858, but because of financial difficulties, it was not until September 1859 that she was ready for her trials.

Brunel, worn out by the burden of his great enterprise and the strain of the long delay over its completion, collapsed aboard her the day before and was still too ill to attend the banquet marking the beginning of her maiden voyage. For some reason that has never been

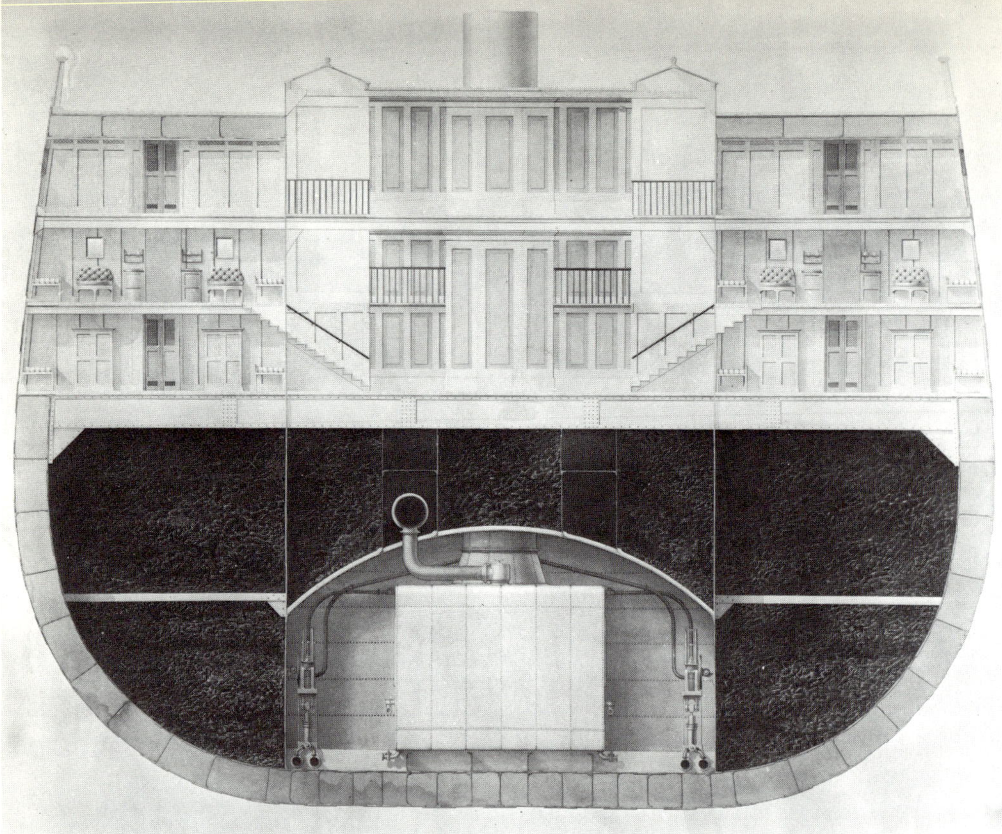

62 Section of *Great Eastern* amidships, showing cellular construction and great bunker capacity

explained, the owners – the Eastern Steam Navigation Company – put her, a ship designed to steam out to Ceylon and back without refuelling, on the relatively short North Atlantic run and she became the most notorious white elephant in nineteenth-century commercial history; but Brunel never knew. He died a week after her first departure.

The giant became a cable ship and in 1865 laid the first transatlantic cable between Valentia in Ireland and Newfoundland, the second one in 1866, the French cable to America in 1869, the Suez–Bombay cable in 1870 and a third Atlantic link in 1873; but she never carried a passenger to Australia and in 1888 was sold to a scrap merchant for £43,000. It was forty years after her launching before another ship so big was laid down.

63 *Great Eastern* beached for the ship-breakers on Merseyside

The P & O SS *Chusan*

While the *Great Eastern* was still a project developing in Brunel's fertile imagination, Arthur Anderson had already established a regular steamer link with Australia. It was an extension of the P & O's Ceylon–Singapore service and provided a ship every two months to King George's Sound, Adelaide, Melbourne and Sydney. The first ship on the run was the iron screw steamer *Chusan*, 699 tons, which sailed at the end of 1852. Calling at Fremantle on the way, she was only the second steamship seen there and the first for seven years. Consequently her arrival caused great excitement and a ball was organized to celebrate the occasion; but, as contemporary local accounts put it, 'she had called quite without purpose', Albany being her destination, and the rejoicing proved premature.

Then Brunel's other and abiding wonder, the *Great Britain* was acquired by the Eagle Line of the Liverpool and Australian SN Company and refitted for the direct Australian trade. Three of her masts and one of her funnels were removed and a two-bladed propeller that could be lifted out of the water installed. She was also given a set of boilers less heavy on fuel and proceeded to make altogether thirty-two voyages to Melbourne, carrying as many as 630 passengers at fifty guineas a head to the Cape, seventy guineas all the way. Her average passage time was about sixty-five days, which was twenty to thirty days better than the best of the clippers.

Meanwhile, the Union Line founded in 1853 had been awarded the contract for the direct mail service between Southampton and Cape Town. This was inaugurated in 1857 by the *Dane*, 580 tons.

The P & O still carried the Australian mail by the Overland Route to Suez, then on via Ceylon and Singapore; but in 1856 the European and Australian Royal Mail Company, mentioned earlier, were given the contract over the head of the older company because of the latter's refusal to accept savage penalty clauses in it. The contract called for a monthly service in return for an annual subsidy of £185,000; but in spite of this and their high hopes, the company failed within two years of its founding, the crash being a famous nineteenth-century business sensation.

The upshot of it all was that the P & O got back their contract and for some time yet all but the wealthiest of the emigrants continued to travel the long way round in the sailing ships of Green of Blackwall, T. & W. Smith and what Lindsay calls 'other private shipowners, long engaged in the trades'.

64 Dockside scene, Melbourne, 1857

6 *The Compound Engine*

THE ONE THING ABOVE ALL ELSE that made it impossible for steamships, even iron ones with screw propellers, to compete with sailing vessels on long passages, was the cost of the coal to run them. For various reasons – increasing demand, the Crimean War and other political factors, coupled with the desire of people in the out-ports to squeeze the maximum profit from the new business of bunkering ships – the price of coal was for ever going up. In 1853, for instance, there was an increase of 50 per cent over the previous year, and the following table gives some indication of the size of this item in the affairs of a large steamship company, in this case the P & O.

Stocks of coal normally held

Port	*Tons*	*Port*	*Tons*
Southampton	2,000	Calcutta	4,000
Malta	5,000	Singapore	8,000
Alexandria and Suez	6,000	Hong Kong	10,000
Aden	20,900	Shanghai	6,000
Bombay	8,000	Yokohama	2,000
Point de Galle	12,000	King George's Sound	4,000
Madras	500	Sydney	1,200

[Lindsay, p. 409]

To keep up these stocks, totalling about 90,000 tons, the company employed no less than 170 sailing ships every year and in the decade 1856 to 1865 inclusive, they spent £5,250,000 on coal alone, an average of just over £500,000 per annum.

SS *Brandon*

Brunel's attempt to solve the problem in a big way with his *Great Eastern* failed; but something had to be done and again, as with the *City of Glasgow* and the screw propeller, it was a smaller and very modest Clyde-built steamer that broke the impasse. She was the *Brandon*, produced by John Elder and Company, a firm subsequently known as the Fairfield Shipbuilding and Engineering Company and the magic in her was her compound engine, brain-child of John Elder and the first ever fitted in a sea-going ship.

Jonathan Hornblower

The compound engine was designed to utilize more efficiently the expansive power of steam. Put at its simplest, it consisted of two cylinders, one smaller in diameter than the other. When it had done its initial stint in the first, or high-pressure cylinder, the steam exhausted into the second or low-pressure one and after doing some more work there, passed out into a separate condenser. The principle was not new. Thurston writes:

> The efficiency to be secured by the expansion of steam had long been known to Watt and he had conceived the idea of economising some of that power, the waste of which was so plainly indicated by the violent rushing of the exhaust steam into the condenser, as early as 1769. . . .

And indeed one of Watt's patents related to the expansion of steam, describing six methods of applying it and 'of equalizing expansive power'. But it was Jonathan Hornblower who in 1781 first patented the compound engine which he developed for pumping out mines. A year later, he built such an engine at Radstock, near Bath. Its high-pressure cylinder was 19 inches in diameter and its low-pressure one, 24 inches. The new machine was apparently successful, but Boulton and Watt brought an action against the inventor for infringement of their patents. It succeeded and Hornblower was imprisoned for defaulting on royalty payments. He died, like so many others involved with the development of the steam engine, 'a disappointed and impoverished man'. His ideas, however, were taken up and modified by others among them Arthur Woolf, a builder of land engines who 'expanded his steam from six to nine times'. Woolf's pumping engines built on the compound principle, were claimed to be over 30 per cent more efficient than those of Watt, raising 40 million lb. one foot high per bushel of coal, against the latter's 30 million.

In spite of these early demonstrations of the superiority of the compound principle, however, its development in marine engines was blocked for half a century. The main reason for this curious time-lag between invention and adoption, was that it demanded the use of higher steam pressures than could be safely generated in the boilers

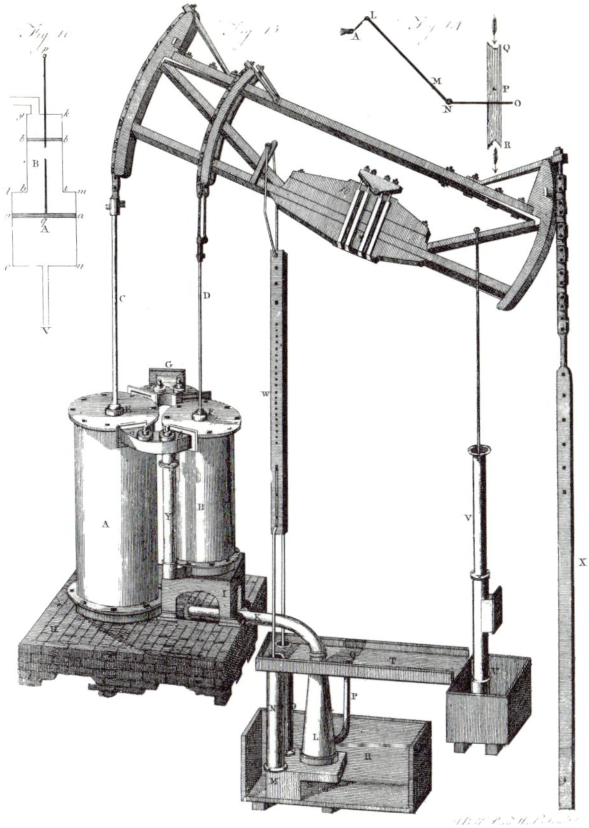

65 Hornblower's compound engine of 1781

used at sea. Building better boilers demanded better tools and techniques than were available, and the surface condenser, so essential for the success of this type of engine, needed looking after with more knowledge, greater skill and a higher degree of dedication than was then generally available in the lower echelons of marine engineering personnel. And finally, there was the old drawback – the conservatism that resisted innovation and regarded every new idea with the gravest suspicion. This attitude was so deeply entrenched that twenty years after the *Brandon* came into service, influential bodies, among them the Admiralty, the United States Coast Survey and the Allan Steamship Company were still trying to decide whether to adopt the new engine or not.

John Elder, 1824–69

Although the credit for the original conception of this revolutionary engine belongs jointly to James Watt and Jonathan Hornblower, it would be difficult to overstate John Elder's contribution to its ultimate development. In 1888, a statue was erected to his memory in Govan Park and at the unveiling it was said:

> ... by his many inventions, particularly in connection with the compound engine, he effected a revolution in engineering second only to that accomplished by James Watt, and in great measure originated the developments in steam propulsion which have created modern commerce. [quoted Smith, p. 178]

Elder's first patent, taken out in the joint names of himself and his partner, Charles Randolph in 1853, described:

> an arrangement of compound engines adapted for the driving of the screw propeller. The engines are vertical, direct-acting and geared. The pistons of the high- and low-pressure cylinders move in contrary directions and drive diametrically opposite cranks with a view to the dimunition of strain and friction. . . . [quoted Smith, p. 178]

The *Brandon* followed and on her trials was found to have a coal consumption of 3¼ lb. per indicated h.p. per hour, compared with the 4 lb. that was usual with simple-expansion engines. Three-quarters of a pound might seem very little to make a fuss about, but it added up to eight tons a day for a ship of 1,000 indicated h.p. and 240 tons for a thirty-day passage. And even so, this was only the beginning. Adjustments and improvements were made and eventually the position was reached where the compound engine working with steam at about 60 lb. per square inch pressure and fitted with surface condensers consumed no more than 2 lb. per indicated h.p. per hour and in some cases even less. Thurston quotes the instance of the United States Revenue steamer, *Hassler*, 151 feet long, 24½ feet beam, 10 feet draught and 125 indicated h.p. which, with steam at 75 lb. pressure, burned only 1·87 lb. at a speed of 7 knots; and Cable records that the P & O's *Mooltan*, 2,257 tons, 1,734 indicated h.p., built in 1861 and equipped with tandem compound engines, burned only 630 tons of coal on her first voyage instead of the current norm of 1,200 tons.

The advantages accruing from the adoption of the compound engine were spelled out for the Institution of Civil Engineers by

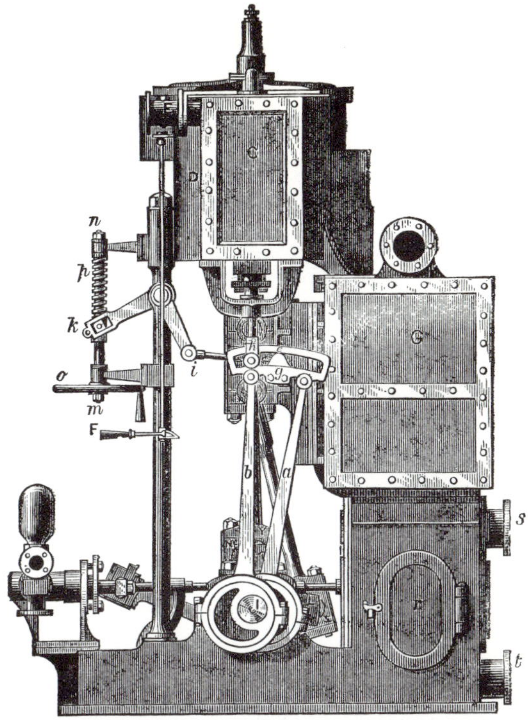

66 John Elder's compound engine, end view

67 Casting a cylinder for a marine engine at Greenwich *c.* 1865.

Richard Bennett in November 1877 as follows:

1 Reduction of the maximum strains in the framing, shafting and bearings and consequent reduction of weight and cost;

2 Increased regularity of turning moment and consequent increased efficiency of the propeller in the water;

3 More economical use of the steam in the cylinder and consequent increase of power from a given expenditure of heat.

[quoted Smith, p. 177]

The first of these was of particular importance in merchant ships, because in plain English it meant that the engines could be built smaller and lighter, leaving more space available for cargo, in addition to that already gained by the reduction in bunker requirements.

Pacific Steam Navigation Company

The first shipping company to take advantage of the new engine was the Pacific Steam Navigation Company, which had been in existence since 1840, trading along the shores of North and South America in the Pacific Ocean, the West Indies and the Atlantic coast of South America. Founded by William Wheelwright an American citizen and one-time United States Consul at Guayaquil, the PSNC began operations with two ships, the *Chile* and *Peru*, which were wooden paddlers of 700 tons gross and 150 h.p. built by Curling and Young of Limehouse. Their big problem was bunkers in the outports. In 1856 with a sizable fleet in operation, they had two new paddle-steamers on order and decided to fit them with compound engines. The ships – the *Inca* and the *Valparaiso* – were so successful and achieved such an economy in fuel, that the company took the extraordinary step of sending three ships already out on the coast, home to be re-engined with compounds. The vessels thus modified were the *Lima*, the *Bogota* and the *Callao*, and Elder subsequently stated that in the *Bogota*, the compound engine using steam at only 25–30 lb. pressure, reduced coal consumption by more than 50 per cent. After that, for the forward-looking at least, the compound engine had arrived and Smith records that by 1866, Randolph and Elder had built 48 sets of them – 18 for paddlers and 30 for screw-propelled steamers, most of them being employed in the Pacific where bunkers were more expensive and a greater worry than anywhere else.

The P & O goes compound

The next big steamer operator to 'go compound' was the giant P & O, who by this time had over fifty liners in service. Most of their building was still done on the Thames and it was the Humphrys tandem version of the compound engine that went into their ships. After the *Mooltan*, mentioned above, came the *Carnatic*, 1,776 tons, 2,442 i.h.p., 27 lb. p.s.i. in 1862, the *Poonah* 2,152 tons, 2,356 i.h.p., 25 p.s.i., and the *Golconda* 1,909 tons, 2,112 i.h.p., 25 p.s.i. in 1863 and the *Baroda* 1,874 tons, 2,486 i.h.p., 27 p.s.i. in 1864. The engines, says Smith,

> . . . were vertical and inverted with two high-pressure cylinders placed above two low-pressure cylinders, driving a two-throw crank-shaft. The stroke was 3 ft. With steam at 26 lb. pressure, the indicated horse-power was 2,442 and the coal consumption under 2 lb. per indicated horse power per hour. [p. 186]

The long-haul freighter

Another owner quick to see the possibilities opened up for steam navigation by John Elder's introduction of the compound engine, was the Ocean Steam Ship Company, now more familiarly known as the Blue Funnel Line and referred to by the always precise W. S. Lindsay, as 'Mr Alfred Holt of Liverpool'. Alfred Holt got into the business about 1855 when he sent out a steamer of '535 tons burden' to trade between Colon and other ports on the Spanish Main. The venture was successful and he expanded rapidly into the China and Far Eastern trades. In 1866, he built three ships – the *Agamemnon*, the *Ajax* and the *Achilles* – which were engined by Scott of Greenock with vertical tandem compound engines, designed to save the maximum weight and space in what were essentially cargo-carriers. On trial, they did everything expected of them and more, and in service were able to steam the 8,500 miles from England to Mauritius without bunkering on the way.

And at this point it may be said that though much remained to be done and greater wonders were still to come, the beginnings – the dreaming and experimenting, the visions and the groping towards them, the heartache and disappointments, the staking and losing – were over. With the compound engine and the advent of the long-haul freighter, the powered ship had come of age and the way ahead for it was wide open.

BIBLIOGRAPHY

Bird, James: *Seaports and Seaport Terminals*, Hutchinson's University Library, London, 1971

Blake, George: *B.I. Centenary*, London, 1957

Bonsor, N. R. P.: *North Atlantic Seaway*, T. Stephenson & Sons Ltd, Prescot, Lancashire, 1955

Bowen, F. C.: *Century of Atlantic Travel, 1830–1930*, 1932

Cable, Boyd: *A Hundred Year History of the Peninsular and Oriental Steam Navigation Company*, Ivor Nicholson and Watson Ltd, London, 1937

Condliffe, J. B.: *The Commerce of Nations*, Allen & Unwin Ltd, London, 1951

Dickinson, H. W.: *James Watt, Craftsman and Engineer*, Cambridge University Press, 1936

Dickinson, H. W.: *Robert Fulton, Engineer and Artist*, John Lane, The Bodley Head, 1912

Gibbs, C. R. Vernon: *Passenger Liners of the Western Ocean*, Staples Press Ltd, London, 1962

Gibbs, C. R. Vernon: *The Western Ocean Passenger Lines and Liners, 1934–69*, Brown, Son & Ferguson Ltd, Glasgow, 1970

Kirkcaldy, Adam W.: *British Shipping. Its History, Organisation and Importance*, Kegan Paul Trench Trubner & Co. Ltd, London, 1914

Lindsay, W. S.: *History of Merchant Shipping and Ancient Commerce*, Sampson Low, Marston, Low and Searle, London, 1876

Muirhead, James Patrick: *The Life of James Watt*, John Murray, London, 1859

Smith, Edgar C.: *A Short History of Naval and Marine Engineering*, University Press, Cambridge, 1937

Spratt, H. Philip: *Transatlantic Paddle Steamers*, Brown, Son & Ferguson Ltd, Glasgow, 1951

Thurston, Robert H.: *A History of the Growth of the Steam Engine*, Cornell University Press, 1878

Waters, Sydney D.: *Clipper Ship to Motor Liner. The Story of the New Zealand Shipping Company, 1873–1939*, NZS Co. Ltd, London, 1939

Wegg-Prosser, Victoria: S.S. *Great Britain*, *Illustrated London News*, London, undated, but *c.* 1970

Woodcroft, Bennet: *A Sketch of the Origin and Progress of Steam Navigation*, Taylor, Walton and Maberly, London, 1848

CONTEMPORARY PERIODICALS

Shipbuilding and Shipping Record
Shipping World and Shipbuilder
Fairplay Shipping Journal
Lloyd's List and Shipping Gazette
The Motor Ship
Modern Transport
Nautical Magazine
Port of London

ACKNOWLEDGEMENTS

The author and publishers wish to extend their grateful thanks to copyright owners for the use of the following pictures:

Thomas Cook & Son Ltd for: 52
Cunard Steam Ship Company Ltd for: 44
John R. Freeman & Co. Ltd for: 64
Mansell Collection for: 6a, 7a, 8, 12, 16, 20, 32, 40, 42, 63, 65
Mary Evans Picture Library for: 4, 6b, 11, 13a, 13b, 14, 15, 17, 19, 21, 22, 26, 30, 31, 55, 58, 60, 66
The National Maritime Museum, Greenwich, London for: 27, 47, 49, 50, 51, 57
The National Portrait Gallery, London for: 24
Paul Popper Ltd for: 37
Radio Times Hulton Picture Library for: 46
The Science Museum, London for: 2, 5, 7b, 9, 10, 18, 23, 25, 28, 29, 33, 34, 36, 38, 39, 41, 43, 45, 53, 54, 56, 62
Shipping World and Shipbuilder for: 3

and for quotations:

Cambridge University Press for Edgar C. Smith: *A Short History of Naval and Marine Engineering*
Cornell University Press for Robert Thurston: *A History of the Growth of the Steam Engine*
Macdonald and Company (Publishers) Limited for W. Lindsay: *History of Merchant Shipping*
Staples Press for C. R. Vernon Gibbs: *Passenger Liners of the Western Ocean*
The London Illustrated News for Victoria Wegg-Prosser: Article on SS *Great Britain*

INDEX

[*Numbers in italics refer to illustrations*]

Printed in Great Britain by Jarrold & Sons Limited, Norwich